Talk Italian

Alwena Lamping

Author and Series editor

Published by BBC Worldwide Ltd
Woodlands, 80 Wood Lane, London W12 0TT
First published 1998
Reprinted 1999, 2000, 2001 (twice)
Reprinted and updated 2002, 2003, 2004

© BBC Worldwide Ltd 1998
ISBN 0 563 400749

Developed by BBC Languages
Edited by Sarah Boas
Additional editing by Tara Dempsey
Design Management by Book Creation Services
Design by Avril Broadley for BCS
Illustrations by Avril Broadley and Beatriz Waller for BCS
Typeset by Avril Broadley for BCS
Production controller Christopher Tinker
Cover design by Carroll Associates
Cover photographs Getty Images (tl, tr, b); The Stock Market
   (back)
Audio producer John Green, TEFL tapes
Sound engineer Tim Woolf
Presenters Aldo Alessio; Jessica Juffré; Massimo Marinoni; Anna-
   Maria Rubino
Studio Robert Nichol Audio Productions
Music by Peter Hutchings

Printed and bound in Great Britain by Martins the Printers Ltd,
   Berwick-upon-Tweed

Contents

Introduction

Welcome to **Talk Italian**, the BBC's new Italian course for absolute beginners. Designed for adults, learning at home or in a class, it provides the ideal introduction to Italian, covering the basic language needed in everyday situations on a visit to Italy. It is suitable if you want to learn for work, for fun and in order to prepare for a first level qualification.

Talk Italian is an interactive course consisting of a book and two 60-minute cassettes or CDs made by native Italian speakers. Although designed to be used with the audio, the book could be used separately as the audio scripts are included in the reference section. Free tutors support and activities are available at http://www.bbcworldwide.com/talk.

Talk Italian encourages you to make genuine progress and promotes a real sense of achievement. The key to its effectiveness lies in its structure and its systematic approach. Key features include:

- simple step-by-step presentation of new language
- involvement and interaction at every stage of the learning process
- regular progress checks
- useful hints on study skills and language learning strategies

How to use Talk Italian

Each of the ten units is completed in ten easy-to-follow steps.

1   Read the first page of the unit to focus on what you are aiming to learn and to note any key vocabulary in the *In Italia* section. This provides useful and relevant information on Italy and sets your learning in context.

2   Listen to the key phrases on the audio – don't be tempted to read them first. Then listen to them again, this time reading them in your book too. Finally, try reading them out loud before listening one more time.

3   Work your way, step by step, through the activities which follow the key phrases. These highlight key language elements and are carefully designed to develop your listening skills and your understanding of Italian. When you hear the activity number, pause the audio and read

the instructions before you listen. To check your answers, refer to the *Audio scripts and answers* starting on page 101.

4   Read the *In italiano* explanations of how the language works as you come to them – they are placed just where you need that information.

5   When you have completed the activities, and before you try the *Put it all together* section, close your book and listen to the Italian conversations straight through. The more times you listen, the more familiar the language will become and the more comfortable you will become with it. You might also like to read the dialogues at this stage.

6   Complete the consolidation activities on the *Put it all together* page and check your answers with the *Audio scripts and answers*.

7   Use the language you've learnt – the presenters on the audio will prompt you and guide you through the *Now you're talking!* page as you practise speaking Italian.

8   Check your progress. First, test your knowledge with the quiz. Then check whether you can do everything on the checklist – if in doubt, go back and spend some more time on the relevant section. You'll have further opportunities to test your knowledge in each *Punto di Controllo* after units 4, 7 and 10.

9   Read the learning hint at the end of the unit, which provides ideas and suggestions on how to use your study time effectively or how to extend your knowledge.

10 Finally, relax and listen to the whole unit, understanding what the people are saying in Italian and taking part in the conversations. This time you may not need the book so you can listen to the audio on its own.

Buona fortuna! Good luck!

Pronunciation guide

The best way to acquire a good Italian accent is to listen to the audio often and to imitate the speakers closely.

1   Italian vowels are consistent and pure sounds.

a	ha		cat
e/è	sette		get
e/é	sera		ace
i	vino	*as in . . .*	meet
o	notte		pot
o	come		pour
u	due		cool

2   Most **consonants** are similar in Italian and English but the following need attention:

			as in . . .
c	+ e or i	cena, ciao	church
	+ all other letters	come, caro	cot
ch		che, chilo	kilo
g	+ e or i	gelato, giorno	jeans
	+ n	signore	canyon
	+ li	famiglia	million
	+ other letters	guida	get
h	always silent	ha	
r	trilled as Scottish r	sera	rose
s		sono	soup
	between two vowels	francese	rise
	+ ce or ci	pesce	ship
	+ c + other letters	scontrino	school
z	has two sounds	zucchero	pads
		pizza	pits

Double consonants are pronounced very emphatically and the sound is prolonged.

3   As a general rule, Italian words are stressed on the last syllable but one, but there are many exceptions which can best be learned gradually by listening. Some words have a written accent to indicate the stress: **città**, **caffè**.

1

Buongiorno!

- saying hello and goodbye
- introducing yourself
- getting to know people

In Italia . . . (In Italy . . .)

greetings tend to be less casual than in many English-speaking countries. When greeting someone and saying goodbye, you often add their name. If you are talking to someone whose name you don't know, you address a man as **signore** and a woman as **signora**. When followed by a surname, **signore** loses its final **-e** to become **signor**.

Saying hello . . .

1   Listen to these key phrases.

Buongiorno   Hello, good morning
Buona sera   Hello, good afternoon/Good evening
Ciao   Hi
Come sta?   How are you?
Bene, grazie . . . Fine, thank you . . .
. . . e lei?   . . . and you?

*Buongiorno,
signore*

2   It's 9 a.m. Listen as Maria Cavalleri, the receptionist
    at the Albergo Giotto, greets people at reception.

    Is the first person she talks to a man or a woman?

    She addresses two people by name.
    Listen and put **signor** or **signora** next to their names.

    .... **Chiesa**
    .... **Riccardi**

3   From mid-afternoon through into the evening, she uses a different
    greeting. Having heard the key phrases, what greeting would you
    expect her to use?

4   Listen as Carla, Giorgio, and some other friends, greet each other in
    the foyer. How many times do you hear **ciao** and **buongiorno**?

    In italiano . . . (In Italian . . .)

    you can use **ciao** (or **buongiorno**) to greet someone you know well.
    To ask how he or she is, you say **Come stai?**

. . . and goodbye

5 Listen to these key phrases.

Arrivederci	Goodbye
Buona notte	Goodnight, goodbye
Ciao	'bye

6 Signor Conti is saying goodbye as he leaves the hotel. Listen out for **buongiorno** which is often used when saying goodbye, to wish someone a nice day. Later in the day **buona sera** can be used in the same way.

7 Angela and Francesca leave next. Listen and fill the gaps in their conversation.

Francesca	.... **Angela** ....
Angela	.... **Francesca** ....

8 It is now late evening and more guests are leaving. How many are men and how many are women?

> Buona notte, signora

9 How would you greet the following people at the times indicated?

9.30 a.m.	signor Calvi, a business acquaintance
5.00 p.m.	Carlo, a good friend
5.00 p.m.	the man giving information in the tourist office
10.00 p.m.	Maria Cavalleri, the hotel receptionist
8.00 a.m.	Lucia, a friend's daughter, who's 12

10 Now try the following. How would you:

- ask signor Calvi how he is?
- ask Carlo how he is?
- say goodbye to signor Calvi?

Introducing yourself . . .

1   Listen to these key phrases.

Io sono . . .   I'm . . .
Lei è . . .   You are . . .

The words **io** (I) and **lei** (you) are often omitted.

2   The receptionist has a problem identifying
    some of the guests arriving at a conference
    in the hotel. Listen and decide if she has
    written down the right names. Correct any
    that are wrong.

    Giovanna Ricci
    Paolo Riccardi
    Enrico Piacenza

3   The next person walks past without checking in. Listen as the
    receptionist asks him who he is and underline the words she uses.

    Maria   **Buongiorno, signore. Signore, lei è . . . ?**
    signor Mancini   **Mancini. Sono Luciano Mancini.**

4   Listen to these key phrases.

    Come si chiama?   What's your name?
    Mi chiamo . . .   My name is . . .
    Piacere   Pleased to meet you
    Scusi?   Excuse me?

5   Listen as Luciano Mancini and Francesca Como meet each other for
    the first time. Tick the key phrases in activity 4 as you hear them.

6   Enrico Piacenza doesn't quite catch Giovanna Ricci's name. How does
    he ask her to repeat it?

. . . and getting to know people

7 Outside the hotel, Mario is also getting to know people. The question
he asks younger people is **'Come ti chiami?'** Listen and complete
the dialogues.

Mario	**Buongiorno. Come si** .... **?**
sig. Lelli	.... **chiamo Franco Lelli.**
Mario	**Ciao.** .... **ti chiami?**
Giulia	.... **chiamo Giulia.**
Mario	**E tu, come ti chiami?**
Marcella	**Mi** .... **Marcella.**

In italiano . . .

lei and **tu** both mean 'you'. You use

> **lei** to someone you don't know well or someone older than
> yourself;
>
> **tu** to a friend, member of the family or a young person.

The choice affects other words:

lei	**Come si chiama?**	**Come sta?**
tu	**Come ti chiami?**	**Come stai?**

If in doubt use **lei**, especially to an older person.

8 Tick any of the following names that you hear in this conversation
in the hotel bar.

Gianna	Gemma	Gregorio	Giorgio
Guido	Giovanna	Geraldo	Giulia

Choose three of the names and work out how these people would
introduce themselves.

Have you noticed that many women's names in Italian end in **-a** while
men's names tend to end in **-o**?

Put it all together

1 Match the English with the Italian.

a	Good night	**Buona sera**
b	Hi	**Arrivederci**
c	My name's	**Come si chiama?**
d	I am	**Ciao**
e	Good morning	**Piacere**
f	How are you?	**Buongiorno**
g	Goodbye	**Mi chiamo**
h	Good evening	**Buona notte**
i	What's your name?	**Io sono**
j	Pleased to meet you	**Come sta?**

2 What could these people be saying to each other?

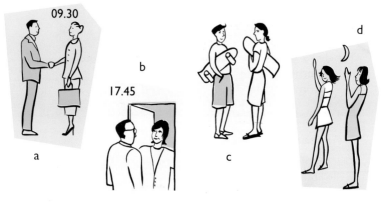

3 The following names are all in this unit. Try saying them out loud, then listen again to the conversations to check your pronunciation.

C before **e** and **i** sounds like **ch** in 'church', but it has a hard **k** sound before all other letters.

Maria Cavalleri	**signora Riccardi**	**signor Conti**
Carla	**Giorgio**	**Franco**
signor Chiesa	**Francesca**	**Enrico Piacenza**
Giovanna Ricci	**Luciano Mancini**	**Marcella**

Now you're talking!

1   Imagine it's lunchtime and you're in the hotel bar at
the Albergo Giotto . . . A man standing by the bar greets you.

◇ **Buongiorno. Come sta?**
◆ Say you're fine; ask how he is.
◇ **Bene, grazie.**

A woman comes in and joins you.

◆ Greet her and introduce yourself.
◇ **Piacere. Io sono Anna Alberti.**
◆ You didn't catch her name. Say 'Excuse me?'
◇ **Anna Alberti.**
◆ Say you're pleased to meet her.

Someone else arrives – you think his name is Luciano
Mironi but you're not sure.

◆ Greet him and ask him if he is Luciano Mironi.
◇ **No, sono Luciano Mancini.**
◆ Say who you are and that you're pleased to meet him.
◇ **Piacere.**

You have to leave.

◆ Say goodbye to Anna and Luciano.
◇ **Arrivederci.**

2   Later, at around 6 p.m., you're in reception.

◆ Greet the receptionist, Maria Cavalleri.
◇ **Buona sera. Come sta?**
◆ Say you're fine. Say hello to her daughter who comes in.
◇ **Buona sera.**
◆ Ask her what her name is.
◇ **Mi chiamo Giulia.**
◆ Ask Giulia how she is.
◇ **Bene, grazie.**
◆ Say goodbye and wish them a nice evening.

Quiz

1 When would you use **Ciao**?
2 What's the Italian for 'Pleased to meet you'?
3 When do you use **Buona sera**?
4 Would you use **tu** or **lei** when speaking to someone you don't know very well?
5 When does **signore** shorten to **signor**?
6 How would you reply if someone asked you **Come sta?**
7 When do you say **Buona notte**?
8 What are the two ways of introducing yourself?
9 In which one of these three names does the letter c have a hard 'k' sound: **Gucci Versace Moschino**?
10 When asking a child's name, would you ask **Come si chiama?** or **Come ti chiami?**

Now check whether you can . . .

☐ greet someone correctly during the day – morning, afternoon and evening

☐ say goodnight and say goodbye

☐ introduce yourself

☐ reply when someone is introduced to you

☐ ask someone's name and give your name

☐ ask someone how they are

☐ reply when someone asks you how you are

☐ ask for clarification if you didn't catch what was said

Listen to the audio as often as you can and try to imitate the people on them as closely as possible. Listening to things over and over again and repeating them many times will help you get familiar with the sounds of Italian. When you practise, say the words and phrases out loud.

Di dov'è?

- talking about where you're from
  . . . and your nationality
- saying what you do for a living
- giving your phone number

In Italia . . .

people tend to be friendly and open, and it is well
worth learning to say a little about yourself and to ask
simple questions, so that you can make conversation
with the Italians you meet.

You'll find many Italians will refer to the town or the
region they come from and say that they are, for
example, **fiorentino** (from **Firenze**, Florence),
romano (from **Roma**), **bolognese** (from **Bologna**),
or **siciliano** (from **Sicilia**).

Talking about where you're from . . .

1   Listen to these key phrases.

(Lei) è inglese?	Are you English? (formal)
(Tu) sei inglese?	Are you English? (informal)
Sì – sono inglese	Yes – I'm English
No – non sono inglese	No – I'm not English
Di dov'è?	Where are you from? **(lei)**
Di dove sei?	Where are you from? **(tu)**
Sono di . . .	I'm from . . .

2   Fiorella, a student doing some market research for an Italian holiday company, talks to a group of English-speaking visitors in Verona. Tick their nationalities as you hear them.

	inglese	australiano/a	americano/a
signora 1			
signore 1			
signore 2			
signora 2			

In italiano . . .

there are two types of adjectives (words which describe, e.g. big, Italian, married, green, this, my).

1 ending in **-e**: **inglese**

2 ending in **-o**: **americano**
   The **-o** changes to **-a** when describing females: **americana**

3   Listen as one of the other students now asks Fiorella about herself. Does he ask **Di dov'è?** or **Di dove sei?**

Which of these northern Italian towns is she from?

Brescia   **Bergamo**   **Bolzano**

. . . and your nationality

4 Can you match these nationalities to the countries? Two have been done for you.

italiano   francese   spagnolo   svizzero   tedesco   australiano
scozzese   gallese   inglese   irlandese   canadese   americano

Paese		Nazionalità
Italia	*Italy*	
Inghilterra	*England*	
Scozia	*Scotland*	
Irlanda	*Ireland*	
Galles	*Wales*	
Stati Uniti	*USA*	*americano*
Australia	*Australia*	
Svizzera	*Switzerland*	
Francia	*France*	
Germania	*Germany*	*tedesco*
Spagna	*Spain*	
Canadà	*Canada*	

Now tick the nationalities which change when describing a woman.

5 Listen to the way some of these countries and nationalities are pronounced and repeat them, taking care to imitate the clear sounds of the vowels – **a e i o u**.

In italiano . . .

è means 'is' and 's/he is' as well as 'you are'.

6 Fiorella tells a colleague about some of the people she interviewed. Listen and fill the gaps.

Antonio è .... **, di Madrid.**
Helen è .... **.**
Mike è di Toronto, è .... **.**
Anna è .... **. È di Edimburgo.**

Saying what you do for a living

1 Listen to these key phrases.

Che lavoro fa?   What do you do? **(lei)**
Che lavoro fai?   What do you do? **(tu)**
Sono infermiera.   I'm a nurse.
Sono in pensione.   I'm retired.
Non sono studente.   I'm not a student.

2 Listen as Fiorella asks three people what they do for a living. Can you work out which one is an engineer, which one a journalist and which one a secretary?

signore ....
signora 1 ....
signora 2 ....

ingegnere
giornalista
segretaria

In italiano . . .

'a' is not used when saying what you do:
Sono casalinga   I'm a housewife
Sono architetto   I'm an architect

3 Fiorella continues with her survey. Listen and fill the gaps with words from the list on the right. What do you think the word **ma** means?

Notice that some occupations have a masculine and a feminine form.

Fiorella **Che lavoro fa?**
         Sono.............. .

Fiorella **Tu sei studente?**
         No, non sono studente.

Fiorella **Che lavoro fai?**
         Sono.............. .

Fiorella **Lei è artista?**
         Sì, ma sono.............. .

professore/essa teacher
ragioniere/a accountant
impiegato/a office worker
direttore manager
guida tour guide
medico doctor
disoccupato/a unemployed

Non sono italiano   I'm not Italian
Non sono ragioniere   I'm not an accountant

Lei non è inglese?   You're not English?
Anna non è casalinga   Anna is not a housewife

4 Fiorella asks another man about his occupation and his nationality.
Make a note of his answers in Italian and English.

lavoro: ....
nazionalità: ....

Giving your phone number

I Look at the following handwritten numbers and note how 1 and 7 are
written. Then listen to the numbers 0 to 10 on the audio.

0   1   2   3   4   5   6   7   8   9   10
zero uno due tre quattro cinque sei sette otto nove dieci

2 Two people give Fiorella their **numero di telefono** (phone number).
Listen and make a note of them.

Gemma   ....
Paolo   ....

3 Say these two phone numbers out loud.

01604 299 385
00 39 51 561 486

Now practise saying your own **numero di telefono**, at home and at
work, and then the numbers of friends and family.

Put it all together

1 Which answer best fits each question?

    a **Signora, lei è inglese?**   **Sono infermiera.**
    b **Lei è italiano, signore?**   **No, io sono romano.**
    c **Di dov'è?**   **No, sono americana.**
    d **Lei è di Firenze?**   **No, non sono italiano.**
    e **Che lavoro fa?**   **Sono di Milano**

2 Marco Manuzzi is an Italian doctor from Florence.
How would he fill in this form? (**Cognome** means surname).

Cognome	....	**Nome**	....
Nazionalità	....		
Professione	....		

3 Fill the gaps in the sentence about Ulrike with:
tedesca   **chiamo**   **dentista**

Mi .... **Ulrike Schmitt. Sono** ...., **di Berlino**

e sono ....

Using the above as your guide,
write what Angela and
Marco would say about
themselves.

Angela Roberts
secretary
Welsh, from Bangor

Marco Blondini
accountant
Italian, from Rome

4 The following places and professions have all been used in this unit.
Can you pronounce them correctly?

Galles Germania Edimburgo giornalista guida ingegnere

g + **e** or **i** sounds like **j** in *jeans,* **gn** sounds like **ny** in *canyon*
gl sounds like **lli** in *million,* **g** + anything else sounds like **g** in *go*

Now you're talking!

I   You are on holiday in Verona and someone asks you where the town hall is. When you tell them you are not from here – **non sono di qui** – it leads to a conversation. You need to know how to:

   ◆ say you're not from here
   ◆ say you're English, from Chester
   ◆ find out where he's from

2   Now imagine you are Andrew Fairlie and play his part in the conversation.

   ◇ **Signor Fairlie, lei è inglese?**
   ◆ *You*
   ◇ **Di dov'è?**
   ◆ *You*
   ◇ **Che lavoro fa?**
   ◆ *You*

   Name: Andrew Fairlie
   Occupation: Architect
   Nationality: Scottish
   Home Town: Edinburgh

3   Still in Verona, you start chatting to someone in your hotel. Listen to the questions and this time answer them with information about yourself.

   ◇ **Buongiorno! Come sta?**
   ◆ *You*
   ◇ **Sono Pietro. Lei, come si chiama?**
   ◆ *You*
   ◇ **Lei è americano?**
   ◆ *You*
   ◇ **Di dov'è?**
   ◆ *You*
   ◇ **Che lavoro fa?**
   ◆ *You*

Quiz

1 Would an Italian woman say **Sono italiano** or **Sono italiana**?
2 How would you tell someone you're from Chester?
3 What are the missing numbers in the sequence?
   due .... **sei** .... **dieci**
4 In a formal working situation, how would you ask someone where they're from?
5 What changes would you make to your question 4 if you were chatting to a young student?
6 How do you say 'I'm not from here' in Italian?
7 Which of the following is the odd one out?
   impiegato canadese tedesco francese
8 If a woman tells you she is **fiorentina**, where is she from?
9 What word would you have to add for this sentence to mean 'I'm not a housewife'? .... **sono casalinga.**

Now check whether you can . . .

☐ say where you're from

☐ say what nationality you are

☐ say what you do for a living

☐ ask others for the above information

☐ use the numbers 0 to 10

☐ give your phone number

To help you to learn new words and phrases you could try listing them in a book, putting them on sticky labels in places where you can't fail to notice them, recording them or getting someone to test you on them – it doesn't have to be an Italian speaker.

Make your vocabulary list relevant to you and your lifestyle – it's much easier to remember words which are important to you.

3

Questo è Paolo

- introducing friends and family
- saying how old you are
- talking about your family

In Italia . . .

the tendency is towards smaller families than in the past, but **la famiglia** (the family) is still the focal point in the lives of most Italians. Don't be surprised to be asked questions about yourself and your family and don't be reserved about asking questions.

The Italians' affection for **bambini** (children) is legendary and they are welcome almost everywhere. You won't have to request special treatment in restaurants since children regularly eat out with their parents, even late into the evening.

Introducing friends . . .

1 Listen to these key phrases.

Questo è . . .   This is (to introduce a man)
e   and
Questa è . . .   This is (to introduce a woman)

2 Mario Grada, who knows many of the conference delegates in the hotel, makes some introductions. Listen, then complete the conversation.

Mario	**Buongiorno, signora Cesare.**
	.... **è Paolo Lega.**
sig. Lega	**Piacere.**
Mario	**E** .... **è Camilla Faldi.**
sig.ra Cesare	**Piacere.**

Piacere

3 Listen to these key phrases.

Questo è mio marito	This is my husband
Questa è mia moglie	This is my wife
Sono sposato/a	I'm married
. . . divorziato/a	. . . divorced

4 Over an informal lunch, Camilla and Paolo introduce their partners to Mario. Listen and tick the right names.

Camilla's husband is	▦ Piero	▦ Pietro
Paolo's wife is	▦ Maria	▦ Marta

5 Some more people join them. Note that they use the informal **tu**. Listen and work out who is married and who isn't.

	Mario	Alessandra	Ettore
sposato/a			
divorziato/a			
single			

. . . and family

6 Listen to these key phrases.

Ha figli?/Ha bambini?	Do you have children?
Ho . . .	I have . . .
. . . un figlio	. . . a son
. . . una figlia	. . . a daughter
Non ho figli	I don't have children

In italiano . . .

uno (one) changes to **un** before a male and **una** before a female; **una** is shortened to **un'** before a vowel: **un'amica** (a friend); **un**, **uno**, **una** and **un'** are also the words for 'a'/'an'.

7 **Figli** (literally 'sons') and **bambini** are both used for 'children' – **bambini** usually for younger children. Listen to Camilla and Marta talking about their children. Do they have sons or daughters?

Mario	**Hai bambini, Camilla?**
Camilla	**Sì, ho .... e ....**
Mario	**E tu, Marta, hai bambini?**
Marta	**Ho .... Roberto! Questo è ....**

8 Mario then talks to Renata.
Is she married?
Does she have children?

ho	I have
hai	you have (**tu**)
ha	you have (**lei**)

9 How would you introduce the following?

- Enrico Piacenza
- Francesca
- your partner

Saying how old you are . . .

1 Listen to some of the following numbers.

11	**undici**	21	**ventuno**	40	**quaranta**
12	**dodici**	22	**ventidue**	50	**cinquanta**
13	**tredici**	23	**ventitré**	60	**sessanta**
14	**quattordici**	24	**ventiquattro**	70	**settanta**
15	**quindici**	25	**venticinque**	80	**ottanta**
16	**sedici**	26	**ventisei**	90	**novanta**
17	**diciassette**	27	**ventisette**	100	**cento**
18	**diciotto**	28	**ventotto**		
19	**diciannove**	29	**ventinove**		
20	**venti**	30	**trenta**		

31 to 99 follow the same pattern as 21 to 29: **trentuno, trentadue, trentatré**, etc.

2 You will hear all but one of the following numbers. Which one is it?
14   100   54   29   36

3 Say the following numbers out loud.
15   55   12   46   87   73

4 Listen to these key phrases.

Quanti anni ha?   How old are you? **(lei)**
Quanti anni hai?   How old are you? **(tu)**
Ho 19 anni   I'm 19

5 Out by the hotel pool, Mario listens to some students chatting.
Listen and note down their ages. **Anch'io** means 'me too'.

Massimo ....

Laura ....

Marianna ....

. . . and talking about your family

statements and questions about a third person are identical to those relating to **lei** (you).

Come si chiama? can mean What's your name?
What's his/her name?

Quanti anni ha? can mean How old are you?
How old is he/she?
How old is . . . ?

The context usually makes the meaning clear.

6 Mario listens to two women talking about their families. Listen and fill the gaps in their conversation.

signora 1	**Lei ha figli?**
signora 2	**Ho una** .... **,Caterina,** **e ho anche un** .... **.**
signora 1	**Come si** .... **?**
signora 2	**Stefano.**
signora 1	**Quanti anni** .... **?**
signora 2	**Ha** .... **anni.**

7 Listen to Anna, Alessandra and Lorenzo introducing their families and decide which family belongs to whom. (**padre** father, **sorella** sister)

a .... b .... c ....

Put it all together

1 **Questa è la famiglia Archenti.**

Look at Sergio Archenti's family tree and choose the correct ending for his statements.

a **Mio padre si chiama**   **Raffaello**   **Roberto**
b **Mia sorella si chiama**   **Daniela**   **Caterina**
c **Isabella è**   **mia madre**   **mia figlia**
d **Isabella ha**   **sedici anni**   **tredici anni**

Are the following **vero** (true) or **falso** (false)?

	vero	falso
e **Daniela è sposata.**		
f **Sergio ha un fratello e un figlio.**		
g **Il fratello di Isabella si chiama Carlo.**		

2 Now read what Sergio says about some of his family:

Mia sorella ha quarantadue anni, anche mio fratello Carlo – sono gemelli.

Can you work out what **gemelli** are?

3 **Ha fratelli?** is the way to ask someone if they have any brothers and sisters. Would you answer **Sì** or **No** if you were asked **Ha fratelli?** and **Ha figli?** If the answer is **Sì,** can you provide more details, giving their names and ages?

Now you're talking!

I   Read these questions and then be guided by the audio.
     Answer as if you were Anna Fraser, married to Jonathan, with two
     children, Sarah (14) and Daniel (12).

Suo and **sua** mean 'your' in this conversation.

◇ **Buongiorno, signora. Come si chiama?**
◆ *You*
◇ **Lei è sposata?**
◆ *You*
◇ **Ha figli?**
◆ *You*
◇ **Come si chiama sua figlia?**
◆ *You*
◇ **Quanti anni ha?**
◆ *You*
◇ **E suo figlio – come si chiama?**
◆ *You*
◇ **Quanti anni ha?**
◆ *You*

2   Now, using the informal **tu**, take part in a conversation with Marco.
     You need to know how to:

◆ say whether you are married or otherwise
◆ ask if he is married
◆ ask if he has children
◆ ask what his daughter's name is
◆ ask how old she is
◆ introduce a friend/partner to him

Quiz

1 Do you need **questo è** or **questa è** to introduce a woman?
2 How would you introduce your brother to Anna?
3 Which of the following means 'my daughter'?
   mio figlio   mia figlia   sua figlia
4 What is the Italian for 'sister'?
5 Does **mio padre** mean 'my mother' or 'my father'?
6 To ask a small child how old s/he is, would you say **Quanti anni hai?**
   or **Quanti anni ha?**
7 Can you say how old you are in Italian?
8 If you're told that someone **ha quindici anni**, are they 5, 15 or 50?

Now check whether you can . . .

  ☐ say whether you are married or otherwise

  ☐ say what family you have

  ☐ give your age

  ☐ ask others for the above information

  ☐ introduce someone – male or female

  ☐ ask or say how old someone else is

  ☐ use the numbers 11 to 100

A good way to practise introducing people is to find a family
photograph with lots of people in it – a wedding group is ideal.
Pointing to each person, say who they are:

e.g. **Questa è mia madre   Questo è mio fratello David**

The following words might come in useful:
nonno, nonna   grandfather, grandmother
cugino, cugina   cousin – male/female
zio, zia   uncle, aunt

4

Un caffè, per favore

- ordering a drink in a bar
- offering someone a drink
  . . . and accepting or refusing

In Italia . . .

you are never very far from a **caffè** or **bar** – they are an important feature of the Italian lifestyle. Open from early morning until late at night, they serve snacks and a wide variety of drinks, hot and cold, alcoholic and soft.

In many bars, you pay at the **cassa** (cash desk), then repeat your order at the bar, handing your **scontrino** (receipt) to the **barista** (barman). It is usual to leave some loose change in the saucer on the bar.

You pay more for drinks brought to you at a table by the waiter than for drinks bought and drunk standing at the bar. The difference in price can be considerable in prime tourist areas.

Ordering a drink . . .

1   Listen to these key phrases.

Prego?/Mi dica	Can I help you?
Un caffè, per favore	A coffee, please
Una birra, per favore	A beer, please
. . . anche per me	. . . for me too
Grazie	Thank you
Prego	You're welcome
Va bene	OK, that's fine

2   Mario orders a beer while waiting in the Bar Roma for some colleagues. Listen out for the strong **r** sound in **birra**.

3   Listen to the family next to him ordering four different drinks. Can you decide who has what?

	un caffè black coffee	un gelato ice cream	una coca coke	un'aranciata fizzy orange
padre	....	....	....	....
madre	....	....	....	....
figlio	....	....	....	....
figlia	....	....	....	....

In italiano . . .

all nouns, not just those referring to people, are either masculine (m.) or feminine (f.)

Nouns ending in **-o** are nearly all m.
  un figlio, un cappuccino

Nouns ending in **-a** are usually f.
  una figlia, una birra, un'aranciata

Some nouns ending in **-e** are m., others are f.
  un padre, un bicchiere (m.)
  una moglie, una notte (f.)

. . . in a bar

4 Listen as other people arrive and order drinks.
What does the man order? ....
How does the woman say she'll have the same? ....
Does the woman have her coffee **con o senza zucchero**
(with or without sugar)?

5 Now listen to a woman ordering drinks for herself and her daughter.
Is the mineral water she orders sparkling (**gassata**) or still (**non gassata**)?
What does her daughter have?

Signora	**Buona sera.**
Cameriere	**Signora, buona sera. Mi dica.**
Signora	**Un'acqua minerale, per favore.**
Cameriere	**Gassata o non gassata?**
Signora	.... **. E un** .... **per mia figlia.**
Cameriere	**Allora, un** .... **e un'acqua minerale** .... **. Va bene.**

6 Anna and Adriano are ordering drinks. Are the following statements **vero o falso** (true or false)?

		vero	falso
a	Anna orders black coffee.		
b	She takes sugar in coffee.		
c	Adriano orders mineral water.		
d	He prefers still water.		

7 How would you ask for:

- a beer?
- a coffee?
- an ice cream?

Offering someone a drink . . .

1 Listen to these key phrases.

Che cosa prende?	What will you have?
Prende un caffè?	Will you have a coffee?
per lei? per te?	for you?
Volentieri	I'd love to/I'd love one
Sì, grazie	Yes please
No, grazie	No thank you
Cin cin!	Cheers!

2 Listen as Mario's colleagues arrive and he offers them coffee.
How does signor Guarino accept? ....
What kind of coffee does Luisa want? ....
(You may need to consult the **In Italia . . .** box.)

In Italia . . .

caffè (or **espresso**) is a small, strong, black coffee
caffelatte is **caffè** with quite a lot of hot milk
cappuccino is **caffè** topped with hot whipped milk
caffè macchiato has just a drop of milk in it
caffè corretto is **caffè** laced with alcohol
caffè lungo is **caffè** in a bigger cup with added water

3 At the **cassa**, Franca buys a drink for Claudia and Fabio. She uses
prendi – the **tu** form of **prende**.
What do they all order? ....
Listen out particularly for the difference in pronunciation between
birra and **birre**.

. . . and accepting or refusing

nouns do not add **-s** to form the plural. Instead, the final vowel changes:

-o and **-e** change to **-i**

un cappuccino	**tre cappuccini**
un bicchiere	**due bicchieri**
una notte	**quattro notti**

-a changes to **-e**

una birra	**due birre**

other letters do not change

un caffè	**tre caffè**
un bar	**due bar**

4 Three people order wine by the glass (**bicchiere**). Tick whether they order **vino rosso** (red wine) or **vino bianco** (white wine).

	vino rosso	vino bianco
Antonio		
Anita		
signora Perrone		

5 Later, Mario is with signor Guarino and an English colleague. Listen out for **Come si dice in italiano 'whisky' ?** (How do you say 'whisky' in Italian?) Do they have their whisky with or without ice (**ghiaccio**)?

	con ghiaccio	senza ghiaccio
signor Howard		
signor Guarini		

What does Mario drink?

Cin cin!

Cin cin!

Put it all together

I   Choose **un**, **una**, **un'** for each item.

.... **caffè**   .... **cappuccino**
.... **tè**   .... **acqua minerale**
.... **vino**   .... **spremuta**
.... **birra**   .... **grappa**
.... **gelato**   .... **frullato**
.... **aranciata**   .... **amaro**

Check the meaning of any new words in the glossary.

2   Rearrange these sentences to form a dialogue.

E tu Fabrizio – prendi un bicchiere di vino?
Allora due caffè e un bicchiere di vino bianco per me.
Volentieri – senza zucchero, per favore.
No grazie – un caffè anche per me.
Buongiorno, Antonia – prende un caffè?

3   The waiter is having difficulty with the orders.
Correct him as in the example, remembering
to change the endings of the words as necessary.

Mi dica

Cameriere   **Un gelato e due caffè?**
You   **No, due gelati e un caffè.**

Una birra e due cappuccini?
a ....

Un cappuccino e due caffè?
b ....

Un caffè e due bicchieri di vino?
c ....

Un'aranciata e due gelati?
d ....

Now you're talking!

I   Imagine you're in a bar in Pisa. You're going to order drinks at the **cassa** for yourself and two Italian friends.

   ◆ Ask Emilio what he'd like to drink.
   ◇ **Un bicchiere di vino bianco, per favore.**
   ◆ Now ask his sister, Francesca, what she'd like.
   ◇ **Un'aranciata, per favore.**

   ◆ At the **cassa**, greet the woman; order a glass of white wine, an orange drink and a beer.

For conversations 2, 3 and 4, make sure you know the words and phrases for the following situations, then close your book and be guided by the audio.

2   ◆ You're offered a coffee.
   ◆ You accept, ask for a cappuccino and say 'without sugar' when asked.

3   Someone has asked what you'd like to drink.
   ◆ You ask what a milk shake is in Italian.

4   ◆ When the waiter arrives, you order two glasses of wine and two beers.

   ◆ When the drinks arrive, thank the waiter. Say 'Cheers!'

If you were in the same **caffè** with your family or colleagues or a group of friends, what drinks would you order for them?

Quiz

1 Which of these is the odd one out?
   zucchero   aranciata   frullato   vino
2 Is coffee with alcohol **caffè macchiato** or **caffè corretto**?
3 If you wanted ice with your drink, would you order **con ghiaccio** or **senza ghiaccio**?
4 What is the plural of **vino**, **birra**, **bicchiere**?
5 What is a **scontrino?**
6 Are nouns ending in **-o** generally masculine or feminine?
7 How do you say 'Cheers!' in Italian?
8 If you order **acqua minerale gassata,** would you get still or sparkling water?
9 What two ways do you know of accepting a drink?
10 How do you say 'You're welcome' in response to **Grazie**?

Now check whether you can . . .

☐ order a drink in a bar

☐ offer someone a drink

☐ accept when someone offers you a drink

   . . . or refuse politely

☐ say whether you want your drink with or without something

☐ ask what something is in Italian

☐ say 'Cheers!'

Bring your Italian learning into your everyday life at every opportunity. Every time you have something to drink, think of the word in Italian. When buying a round of drinks, try to memorize the list in Italian.

In a restaurant, bar or supermarket, see how many drinks you can name in Italian.

1 Listen to one of Fiorella's interviews for her survey, then tick the right
information. Listen out for her first question:
Lei è qui in vacanza o per lavoro? Are you here on holiday or for
work?

Laura Santoro è in Italia	in vacanza	per lavoro
Laura è	italiana	americana
Suo padre è	italiano	americano
È in Italia con	sua nonna	suo padre
È di	San Diego	Santiago
È	sposata	divorziata
Ha	due figli	un figlio
È	casalinga	disoccupata

2 While waiting at the airport, you overhear two students getting to
know each other. Listen to their conversation and fill in the missing
details.

nome	nazionalità	età (age)	fratelli/sorelle
Caterina	....	....	....
Jonathan	....	....	....

3 Caterina and Jonathan decide to have a drink together and go to the
bar. Make a note of what they have to drink and the phone numbers
which they exchange.

	un bicchiere di . . .	numero di telefono
Caterina	....	....
Jonathan	....	....

4 Practise pronouncing the names of these Italian wines, then check
your pronunciation with the audio.

Chianti	Frascati	Valpolicella	Barbaresco
Tocai	Verdicchio	Bardolino	Barolo
Lambrusco	Montepulciano d'Abruzzo		Soave

5 Listen to some of the interim results from the Eurovision Song Contest being read out and fill in the missing numbers.
Can you guess what all the countries are?

Danimarca	19	Lussemburgo	
Grecia	75	Norvegia	
Irlanda		Olanda	
Israele		Portogallo	

A good way to practise low numbers is to throw two dice and say aloud all the possible number combinations:

uno
cinque
quindici
cinquantuno

6 Choose the right expression.

a Accepting a drink.
b In reply to **grazie**.
c You haven't heard something properly.
d You're introduced to someone.
e In reply to **Come sta?**
f Saying 'Cheers!'

7 The hotel **padrone** (proprietor) has asked if you would help his cousin fill in a form for an English course in London.
What are the questions you would need to ask her before you could fill in the missing entries?

Name	....
Address	Via Gramsci 23, 41100 MODENA ....
Telephone no.	059 933121 ....
Age	....
Nationality	Italian ....
Occupation	....

a ....

b ....

c ....

8 Fill the gaps in these sentences.

Una _ _ _ _ _ per favore

_ _ _ _ _ _ è Giorgio

Che _ _ _ _ _ _ fa?

Mia _ _ _ _ _ _ ha 85 anni

Sono _ _ _ _ _ _ _, di Bath

_ _ _ _ _ anni hai?

_ _ _ _ rosso o bianco?

_ _ _ _ _ un caffè?

_ _ _ zucchero?

_ _ _ _ sta?

What is the word in the shaded column?

9 A neighbour asks for your help when her daughter receives a letter in Italian from a penfriend.

Translate the first page of the letter for them. Some words and expressions are given underneath; any other new vocabulary can be found in the glossary.

Siracusa

Cara Rachel,

mi chiamo Alessandra Giardi e sono siciliana, di Siracusa. Ho quattordici anni.

Siamo cinque in famiglia – mio padre, Massimo, che è disoccupato; mia madre, Giuseppina, che è infermiera all'ospedale; e mio fratello Stefano, che è studente. Stefano ha diciannove anni. C'è anche mia nonna,

siamo cinque we are five, there are five of us
all' at the
che who
c'è there is

Don't worry too much about making mistakes. You'll learn much more quickly if you try and express yourself, even if you make a few mistakes, than if you say nothing until you are word perfect.

You can give yourself time to think by using words such as **allora** (right, well then) or **vediamo** (let's see).

Scusi, dov'è la stazione?

- asking where something is
- asking for help to understand
- talking about where you live and work

In Italia . . .

the focal point of many Italian towns is **il centro storico** (the old town). Narrow streets and beautiful old buildings still remain much as they were centuries ago. In some towns, historic buildings house contemporary institutions such as **il municipio** (the town hall), **l'azienda di turismo** (the tourist office), **la Camera di Commercio** (the Chamber of Commerce) or **la questura** (the police headquarters).

Asking where something is . . .

1 Listen to these key phrases.

Scusi	Excuse me
Dove?	Where?
Dov'è il duomo?	Where is the cathedral?
È lontano?	Is it far?
. . . dieci minuti a piedi	. . . 10 minute walk

2 Mario asks his friend Anna to point out some local landmarks on his map. First check the meanings of the words using the glossary.

Azienda di turismo · Corso Vittorio · Viale · Teatro Emanuele · Via Puccini · Questura · Stazione · Michelangelo · Duomo · Municipio · Via della Vittoria · Ufficio postale · Piazza Garibaldi

Now listen and match the buildings with the phrases below.

a **qui** (here)   *b* **dietro** (behind) **il municipio**
c **lì** (over there)   *d* **in via** (street) **della Vittoria**
                         e **in centro città** (in the town centre)

In italiano . . .

the words for 'the' in the singular are . . .

masculine	**il**	**centro**	before a consonant
	l' {	**ufficio**	before a vowel or **h**
		hotel	
	lo	**studio**	before **z** or **s** + consonant
feminine	**la**	**stazione**	before a consonant
	l'	**agenzia**	before a vowel

. . . and asking for help to understand

3 Listen to these key phrases.

Può ripetere, per favore?	Can you repeat that, please?
Può parlare lentamente?	Can you speak slowly?
Dove sono i negozi?	Where are the shops?
. . . a duecento metri	. . . 200 metres away
. . . a cinquecento metri	. . . 500 metres away

4 Listen as Mario is stopped in the street by someone looking for **il municipio** (the town hall). She finds it difficult to understand his reply. Assuming she understands English, can you interpret for her?

Visitor	**Può parlare lentamente?**
Mario	**È in centro, lontano da qui . . . venti minuti a piedi.**

5 Listen to someone asking where **i negozi** (the shops) are. How does she ask 'where are . . . ?'

Listen again and make a note of these key points from the answer: Where are they and how far away? How long will it take to walk there?

In italiano . . .

the words for 'the' in the plural are:

masculine	**i**	**negozi**	before a consonant
	gli {	**uffici**	before a vowel or
		studi	before **z** or **s** + consonant
feminine	**le** {	**piazze**	before a consonant
		aziende	before a vowel

---

6 How would you ask where the following are?

- the tourist office
- the post office
- the station
- the shops

Talking about where you live . . .

1 Listen to these key phrases.

Dove abita? — Where do you live?
Abita qui? — Do you live here?
Abito . . . — I live . . .
. . . a Bologna — . . . in Bologna
. . . in centro — . . . in the centre
. . . in periferia — . . . in the suburbs
. . . in campagna — . . . in the country

2 Mario asks some of the people he meets in Bologna where they live.
Listen and tick who lives where.

	in centro	in periferia	in campagna
signora 1			
signore			
signora 2			

3 Later, others talk to him about their homes. Listen and make a note of
the numbers missing here from their addresses. In Italy, the number is
usually written after the street name.

Claudia Bonino   **Viale Roma,** ....
Riccardo Quarta   **Piazza Garibaldi,** ....
Caterina Galli   **Via Verdi,** ....
La figlia di Caterina **Via Aurelia,** ....

4 Listen again to the last conversation, this time making a note of what
type of house they all live in.

un appartamento (flat)   **un palazzo** (block of flats)
una casa (house)   **una villetta** (small detached house)

5 How would you say what type of house you live in and where it is?

. . . and work

6 Listen to these key phrases.

Dove lavora?	Where do you work? **(lei)**
Dove lavori?	Where do you work? **(tu)**
Lavoro . . .	I work . . .
Non lavoro	I don't work

7 Listen to Mario talking to Caterina Galli and her children Franca and Luciano. Decide who works:

in un ufficio (in an office) ....

per la Zanussi (for Zanussi) ....

to show *who* is doing something you change the verb ending, instead of using words for 'I', 'you', 'he', etc.

	abitare (to live)	**lavorare** (to work)	**prendere** (to take)
I	**abito**	**lavoro**	**prendo**
you (**tu**)	**abiti**	**lavori**	**prendi**
you (**lei**)	**abita**	**lavora**	**prende**
he/she	**abita**	**lavora**	**prende**

A very large number of Italian verbs end in **-are** and follow the same pattern as **abitare** and **lavorare**.

To say I, you, we, *don't* do something, you simply put **non** before the verb.

8 Listen as five people answer the question **Dove lavora?** and number their answers 1 to 5 as you hear them. Can you work out what the fifth person does?

Lavoro in un ufficio   A Roma

Lavoro per la Fiat   Non lavoro

In una pizzeria in centro

Put it all together

1 Fill the gaps with the correct form of 'the' – **il, la, l', i, gli** or **le**.

a .... **duomo** .... **negozi** .... **casa**
b .... **stazione** .... **azienda** .... **appartamento**
c .... **vino** .... **acqua** .... **birra**
d .... **madre** .... **padre** .... **bambini**

2 Match the answers to the questions.

a **Dov'è la stazione?** **Cinque minuti a piedi.**
b **Dove lavora?** **È in centro.**
c **Abita qui?** **Sono in centro.**
d **Dove sono i negozi?** **No, lavoro in centro.**
e **Lavora in periferia?** **Lavoro in via Marconi.**
f **Il museo è lontano?** **Sì, abito qui.**

3 In the last four pages there are examples of both **a** and **in** used with places to mean 'in'. Can you work out which you would use with the following?

a .... **Firenze** e .... **un negozio**
b .... **piazza Garibaldi** f .... **una pizzeria**
c .... **Milano** g .... **un ufficio**
d .... **via Manzini** h .... **Roma**

4 Rearrange the letters to find the following:

a a home OMRATPNPAAET
b a number UOTEEDNC
c a civic building OIUCIMNPI
d a word for 'the' IGL
e part of a town AFERRIPIE

Now you're talking!

1   Before leaving your hotel to see the city, you ask the receptionist where a few places are.

    ◆ Greet her and ask where the Cathedral is.
    ◇ **Il Duomo? È in centro – in piazza Duomo.**
    ◆ Ask if it's far.
    ◇ **No, no, dieci minuti a piedi.**
    ◆ Now ask her where the town hall is.
    ◇ **È dietro il Duomo.**
    ◆ You didn't quite catch that. Ask her to repeat what she said.

2   ◆ Later, in the town hall, ask the man at the entrance where the shops are.
    ◇ **Sono in via Michelangelo, a due passi.**
    ◆ Ask him to speak more slowly.
    ◇ **In via Michelangelo, a due passi . . . non è lontano.**
    ◆ Thank him.

3   He asks you some questions. You might like to prepare your answers and then be guided by the audio. You'll need to know how to say:

    ◆ what nationality you are, and which town you live in
    ◆ whether you live in the town centre or out of town
    ◆ if you have a job, what you do and where you work

4   You chat a little longer.

    ◆ Ask him if he lives here.
    ◇ **No, lavoro qui ma abito in via Belloni.**
    ◆ Ask where via Belloni is.
    ◇ **Non è lontano – è in periferia, a quindici minuti da qui.**

Quiz

1. Is **qui** or **lì** the Italian for 'here'?
2. What's the difference between **dov'è?** and **dove sono?**
3. If something is **dietro la stazione**, is it near, behind or opposite the station?
4. To say someone lives in the suburbs, would you say **abita in periferia** or **abita in centro**?
5. What are the words for 'the' before   **birra   figlio   Italia**?
6. What is the **centro storico** of an Italian town?
7. If 200 is **duecento** and 500 is **cinquecento**, what is the Italian for 400?
8. To say 'I don't live here' what word is missing from the sentence .... **abito qui**?

Now check whether you can . . .

☐ ask where something is

☐ ask if it's far

☐ ask someone to repeat something

☐ ask someone to speak slowly

☐ say where you live and where you work

☐ ask someone where they live and work

Learning language patterns (i.e. grammar) allows you to manipulate a language and to say what you want to say without relying on set phrases.

Parlare is the Italian for 'to speak' and it follows exactly the same pattern as **abitare** and **lavorare**. So, to say what languages you speak, you use **parlo** followed by the language, for example: – **parlo inglese, non parlo francese.** The Italian words for languages are the same as the words for masculine nationalities on page 17.

C'è una banca qui vicino?

- understanding what there is in town
  . . . and when it's open
- making simple enquiries
- understanding directions

In Italia . . .

when arriving in a town for the first time, it is always worth visiting the local **azienda di turismo** (tourist information office), where you will be given a free **piantina** (map) and comprehensive information on local amenities, events and places of interest.

Look out for the **ENIT** sign, the logo of the Italian State Tourist Board, or **APT (Azienda di Promozione Turistica)**.

Understanding what there is in town .

1   Listen to these key phrases.

Ecco . . .	Here's . . .
C'è . . .	There is . . .
Non c'è . . .	There isn't . . .
Ci sono . . .	There are . . .
molti, molte	many (m.pl./f.pl.)

2   Can you match the Italian words below with the English equivalents?
Many are very similar and you will probably be able to guess
the meaning, others you may have to look up in the glossary.

una trattoria – small family restaurant

una banca	**un museo**
un albergo	**una piscina**
un mercato	**una farmacia**
una stazione	**un teatro**
un supermercato	**un ristorante**

market
restaurant
theatre
supermarket
chemist's
swimming pool
bank
station
hotel
museum

In italiano . . .

ne means 'of them'
ce n'è uno/a 'there is one (of them)'

3   Caterina Bossoli at the **azienda di turismo** tells visitors about some
of the amenities **in città** (in town). She mentions several of the places
from the list above. Listen and tick them as you hear them.

4   Listen again to Caterina and then decide whether the following are
vero or **falso**.

	vero	falso
a **C'è una piscina.**		
b **C'è un teatro.**		
c **Il mercato è in centro.**		
d **Ci sono molti ristoranti.**		

. . . and when it's open

5 Listen to these key phrases.

È aperto	It's open
È chiuso	It's closed
oggi	today
ogni giorno	every day
ogni lunedì	every Monday

lunedì (Mon)	**giovedì** (Thurs)
martedì (Tue)	**venerdì** (Fri)
mercoledì (Wed)	**sabato** (Sat)
	domenica (Sun)

6 In the **azienda di turismo**, Mario gains some useful information about local places as he waits in a queue. Listen and fill in the gaps.

La piscina è aperta ....

.... e .... c'è un mercato in **Piazza Marconi** in centro.

Il museo è chiuso .... ; è aperto .... , ... e
....

L'azienda di turismo è chiusa ....

In italiano . . .

when describing places or objects, adjectives have to be masculine or feminine to agree with what they describe.

Il museo è apert<u>o</u>.   **La piscina è apert<u>a</u>.**

Making simple enquiries . . .

1 Listen to these key phrases.

C'è . . . ?	Is there . . . ?
C'è una banca qui vicino?	Is there a bank near here?
Ci sono ristoranti?	Are there any restaurants?
Quando?	When?
Mi dispiace	I'm sorry
Non lo so	I don't know

sempre dritto

a sinistra   **a destra**

2 Listen as Anna asks in the bar if there's a phone and a toilet.
Tick the boxes which show where they are.

	qui	lì	in fondo (at the end)	a destra	a sinistra
il telefono					
la toilette					

3 Later, she needs **una banca**. The first person she asks isn't from the area. How does he say he doesn't know?

4 She tries again. Listen out for **poi** (then).
Should she go left or right first?

5 Next, the chemist's. Listen and make a note in English of the instructions. Listen out for **la prima a destra** (first on the right).

....

....

. . . and understanding directions

6 Listen as she then decides to find the **azienda di turismo**.

Where is it?
Is it open today?
What number **autobus** (bus) could she take?

7 Anna decides to walk and asks again for directions. Listen as she's given two instructions.

How far is it to the **semaforo** (traffic lights)?
Should she turn right or left at the lights?

8 **L'azienda di turismo è aperta.** Anna asks about markets, museums, swimming pools and **magazzini** (department stores). Listen and choose **vero** or **falso** for each of the following.

		vero	falso
a	**C'è un mercato ogni giorno.**		
b	**Ci sono due musei.**		
c	**I musei sono chiusi domenica.**		
d	**La piscina è aperta mercoledì.**		
e	**I magazzini sono in centro.**		
f	**I magazzini sono chiusi giovedì.**		

In italiano . . .

like nouns, adjectives have plural endings, both m. and f.
I musei sono aperti
Le piscine sono aperte
Ci sono molti ristoranti e molte pizzerie

9 How would you ask if there's one of the following nearby?

- bank
- chemist's
- restaurant
- supermarket

Put it all together

1 Read the following notices and answer the questions.

GALLERIA D'ARTE MODERNA

Via Flaminia, 16
aperta ogni giorno 9.00–19.00
domenica 9.00–13.00

APT

Azienda di Promozione Turistica
ogni giorno 9.00–13.30; 15.45–19.00

CENTRO DELLA CERAMICA

Via S. Margherita, 4
Orario: 9.30–13.30
Chiuso martedì
Ingresso gratuito

MUSEO ARCHEOLOGICO

Da martedì a sabato 9.00–17.00
domenica 9.00–12.00
lunedì chiuso
Ingresso € 3,00

a On which day is the Archeological Museum closed?
b Is the Gallery of Modern Art open on Sundays?
c When is the tourist office open?
d On which day is the Ceramics Centre closed?

2 Using **c'è**, **non c'è**, **ci sono** and **non ci sono**, can you say which of the amenities mentioned in this unit there are in your home town?

e.g. **C'è un teatro. Non c'è una piscina.**

You might need **un cinema**, which is m. even though it ends in -**a**.

3 And can you say in Italian which days the following in your town are open and closed?

a bank   *b* library (**biblioteca**)   *c* post office

Now you're talking!

I   **In città**, you ask for some information from a man at the bus stop.

   ◆ Say 'Excuse me' and ask if there's a chemist's nearby.
   ◇ **Una farmacia . . . Sì, a sinistra poi sempre dritto.**
   ◆ Repeat the directions you were given and thank him.

2   This time you stop a woman who's passing.

   ◆ Say 'Excuse me' and ask if there's a supermarket here.
   ◇ **C'è l'ipermercato a Molinella . . . ma è lontano.**
   ◆ Ask if there's a bus.
   ◇ **Sì, deve prendere il numero quarantadue.**
   ◆ Repeat the number of the bus, thank her and say goodbye.

3   Imagine you've just arrived in Florence on the train.

   ◆ Ask if there's a bar nearby.
   ◇ **Lì a sinistra – ecco.**
   ◆ Say 'thank you' and ask if there's a hotel nearby.
   ◇ **Mi dispiace, non lo so.**
   ◆ Ask where the tourist office is.
   ◇ **A destra, sempre dritto duecento metri, poi la prima
     a sinistra.**
   ◆ Repeat the instructions then ask if it's open.
   ◇ **Sì, sì.**

4   Later you look for somewhere to eat.

   ◆ Ask if there are any restaurants nearby.
   ◇ **In via Doria c'è la Trattoria Corallo.**
   ◆ Ask if it's far.
   ◇ **No, no, cinque minuti a piedi.**

Quiz

1   What would you expect to find in a building with an **APT** logo on it?
2   If someone told you to go **a destra**, would you go left or right?
3   Can you name two eating places in Italian?
4   How would you ask if there's a phone?
5   If the **azienda di turismo** is **chiusa**, is it open or closed?
6   To ask if there's a supermarket, would you use **c'è** or **ci sono**?
7   Which two days of the week do not end in **-dì** in Italian?
8   What is **una piantina**?
9   How would you say you don't know?

Now check whether you can . . .

- tell someone what there is in a town

- ask if something is available

- understand some straightforward directions

- ask if a place is open or closed

- say you're sorry

- say you don't know

- recognize the names of the days of the week

Learning a new language often involves guessing the meaning of words.
Many Italian and English words derive from the same root, which
makes it relatively easy to guess at their meaning with some
confidence.

If **stazione** means 'station' and **comunicazione** means
'communication', what do you think **nazione**, **tradizione** and
conversazione mean?

Guessing, of course, is not always successful, but it's usually well
worth a try.

Quanto costa?

- understanding prices
- asking for items in a shop
- shopping for food in the market

In Italia . . .

you will find a tremendous variety of places to shop ranging from bustling open-air markets for fresh produce to exclusive boutiques selling designer labels. Italy is famous particularly for fashion, leather goods, ceramics, wine and olive oil. Shops are generally open from Monday to Saturday, from 9 a.m. to 1 or 1.30 p.m. and then from 4 p.m. until around 7.30 p.m.

La tabaccheria (the tobacconist's) sells tickets for buses, trams and the metro, as well as the usual range of tobacco products.

Understanding prices . . .

1 Listen to these prices in euros. You'll hear that **euro** does not change in the plural but that **centesimo** changes to **centesimi**.

€ 1,00	**un euro**	€ 3,99	**tre euro e novantanove**
€ 0,01	**un centesimo**	€ 50,00	**cinquanta euro**
€ 0,20	**venti centesimi**	€ 100,00	**cento euro**
€ 2,00	**due euro**	€ 250,00	**duecentocinquanta euro**

In Italia . . .

the currency is the **euro €. 1 euro = 100 centesimi**. Prices are written with a comma between euros and centesimi: for example, € 12,20 is said as **dodici euro e venti**.

2 Make a note in the spaces of the six prices you hear.

a € ....   *b* € ....   *c* € ....
d € ....   *e* € ....   *f* € ....

3 Listen to these key phrases.

Dica/Mi dica	Can I help you?
Quanto costa?	How much is (it)?
questo/questa	this (m.)/(f.)
Quanto costano?	How much are (they)?
Avete . . . ?	Have you got . . . ?
Prendo . . .	I'll take . . .

4 Here is a list of items Mario needs from the **farmacia** (chemist's), the **tabaccheria** and the **edicola** (newspaper kiosk). Can you find out what they are, using the glossary?

guida di Firenze
3 cartoline
giornale inglese
3 francobolli
carta telefonica
cerotti

. . . and asking for items in a shop

5 Listen and complete the conversation in the **edicola**.

Commessa	**Buongiorno. Dica.**
Mario	**Signora, quanto** .... **questa guida?**
Commessa	.... **euro.**
Mario	**E quanto** .... **i giornali inglesi?**
Commessa	.... **e** .... **.**

6 Before listening to Mario in the **farmacia**, decide how you think he will ask how much the plasters cost.

7 Next, to the **tabaccheria** to buy postcards and stamps for Britain and for the USA. Listen and find out how much things cost, then select the right answers.

una cartolina	un francobollo per la Gran Bretagna	un francobollo per gli Stati Uniti
€0,30	€0,40	€0,50 ....
€0,41	€0,41	€0,51 ....
€0,50	€0,49	€0,52 ....

8 Listen as Mario buys some **biglietti per l'autobus** (bus tickets).

How much is one ticket?
How many does he buy?
How much change (**resto**) is he given?

9 How would you ask if the shop has:

- stamps?   - a guide?   - bus tickets?

. . . and how would you ask the price of:

- a postcard?   - bus tickets?   - an English newspaper?

Shopping for food . . .

formaggio

zucchero 1kg

olio

acqua

vino

mezzo chilo   **un chilo**   **mezzo litro**   **un litro**   **una bottiglia**

panini

prosciutto

sei   **100 grammi/un etto**

una bottiglia di vino rosso
un litro di acqua minerale (gassata)
mezzo litro di olio di oliva (extra vergine)
un chilo di zucchero
mezzo chilo di formaggio
un etto di prosciutto
6 panini

1 Mario meets a friend, Barbara Gelli, shopping for food. Read her shopping list, then, as she tells Mario what she's going to buy, tick off the items.

She mentions one extra item.
Can you add it to the list?

2 Listen to these key phrases.

Mi dà . . .	Could you give me . . . ?
Vorrei . . .	I'd like . . .
questi/queste	these (m.)/(f.)
Altro?	Anything else?
Basta così?	Is that all?
Basta	That's enough/that's all

3 Listen as signora Gelli buys things from the various stalls and make a note of what she buys. After listening several times, match your list with the original one above. What hasn't she bought yet?

. . . in the market

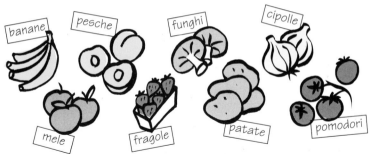

banane · pesche · funghi · cipolle · mele · fragole · patate · pomodori

4 She then goes to buy **frutta e verdura** (fruit and vegetables). Listen and decide what quantities of the following she buys:

- apples
- mushrooms
- tomatoes

5 While waiting for Barbara, Mario listens to the people around him shopping. Listen too and fill the gaps.

- **Vorrei mezzo chilo di questi** ....

- **Prendo** .... **banane.**

- **Mi dà** .... **di patate.**

- **Una di queste** .... **per favore.**

6 Finally, listen as Barbara checks whether she has remembered everything before going home. Has she got all the following?

- wine
- mineral water
- bread rolls
- ham
- cheese

What has she bought which was not on the original list?

7 How would you ask for:

- ¹/₂ kg. of these apples?
- three peaches?
- a litre of mineral water?
- a bottle of red wine?

Put it all together

1 Match the English with the Italian phrases:

a	**Vorrei**	How much is it?
b	**Mi dà**	That's all
c	**Basta così**	How much are they?
d	**Quanto costa?**	Do you have?
e	**Avete?**	Could you give me?
f	**Altro?**	I'd like
g	**Quanto costano?**	Anything else?

2 The following ingredients for **pizza margherita** and for **macedonia** (fruit salad) have been mixed up. Separate them into the two columns – seven items in each.

	pizza margherita	macedonia
fragole, arance, pomodori, funghi, zucchero, patate, pesche, formaggio (mozzarella), banane, mele, sale, pepe, olio di oliva, farina, limone	....	....
	....	....
	....	....
	....	....
	....	....
	....	....
	....	....

Which ingredient is left over?

3 You are shopping for a picnic lunch – you want:

bread rolls, cheese, ham, tomatoes, bananas, apples, two bottles of wine and a bottle of mineral water.

Write your shopping list in Italian.

4 If you buy three items each costing the following, and pay for them all with a 50 euro note, how much change should you expect?

diciotto euro
quattordici euro e venticinque
dieci euro e settantacinque

Now you're talking!

Imagine you are in the market in Bologna, buying a picnic lunch.

1   First, **frutta e verdura**.

  ◇ **Buongiorno. Dica.**
  ◆ Ask for a kilo of apples and half a kilo of bananas.
  ◇ **Altro?**
  ◆ You want half a kilo of tomatoes.
  ◇ **Basta?**
  ◆ Say yes, that's all and thank him.

2   In the **alimentari** (grocer's) . . .

  ◆ Ask for four bread rolls.
  ◇ **E poi?**
  ◆ Say you'd like a bottle of red wine and a litre of sparkling mineral water.
  ◇ **Altro?**
  ◆ You'd like 100 grams of ham.
  ◇ **Quale?**
  ◆ He's asking which one. Say 'this one here'.
  ◇ **Basta così?**
  ◆ Say that's all and thank him.

3   Then you go to the **tabaccheria**. Read the following notes, then close your book and be guided by the audio. You will need to:

  ◆ ask how much a stamp for Britain costs
  ◆ say you'll take two postcards and two stamps
  ◆ ask how much bus tickets cost
  ◆ buy six tickets
  ◆ ask for a telephone card

Quiz

1　Would you use **Quanto costa?** or **Quanto costano?** to ask the price of: **le mele**, **i cerotti**, **una bottiglia di vino**?
2　How much is **cinquecentocinquantacinque**?
3　How many **etti** are there in a **chilo**?
4　Where can you buy bus tickets?
5　If **un giornale inglese** is an English newspaper, what is the Italian for an Italian newspaper?
6　How would you ask for a stamp for Australia?
7　To say 'these tomatoes', do you need **questi** or **queste**?
8　What word would you add to say 'half a kilo': .... **chilo**?

Now check whether you can . . .

▢　ask how much something costs

▢　understand the answer

▢　say you'd like something or you'll take something

▢　give some detail of what you want to buy,
　　e.g. ask for a kilo, half a kilo, 100 grams of food,
　　a bottle, a litre, half a litre of a liquid

▢　ask for stamps for a particular country

Looking things up in a dictionary can be more complicated than using the glossary and it is useful to know some basic grammatical terms and abbreviations. You'll find something like this:

orange 1 n. *(fruit)* arancia f.; *(tree)* arancio m.; 2 adj. *(colour)* arancione
organize v. organizzare

Key: n. = noun, f. = feminine, m. = masculine, adj. = adjective, v. = verb.

I Listen to three people in the **azienda di turismo** being given directions. Follow their route on the map, then write down the place they're looking for and the letter which corresponds to it on the map.

a ....   b ....   c ....

2 Look at the map again and decide which word fits in the gap in each sentence.

azienda di turismo   edicola   bar   farmacia

a **C'è un** .... **e un'** .... **in piazza Italia.**

b **L'** .... **è a sinistra del mercato.**

c **La** .... **è fra la banca e l'ufficio postale.**

3 Listen to the assistant in the **azienda di turismo** telling someone how far various Italian cities are from Milan, and fill in the distances.

Roma	....	**km. da Milano**
Firenze	....	**km.**
Napoli	....	**km.**
Bari	....	**km.**

4 Listen and check whether the prices you hear are the same as the ones on the list. Tick the ones that are correct and change the ones which are wrong.

100g. prosciutto di Parma	€3,60
1 litro olio di oliva extra vergine	€8,95
100g. olive	€2,25
½ kg pomodori	€0,90
pane integrale	€1,00
250g. mozzarella	€3,79

5 Match each sentence to the place in which you're most likely to hear it.

Farmacia   Tabaccheria   Azienda di turismo
Mercato   Caffè   Edicola

a **Quanto costano i giornali inglesi?**
b **Mi dà mezzo chilo di mele.**
c **Avete aspirina?**
d **Vorrei tre francobolli.**
e **È aperto oggi il museo?**
f **Due birre, per favore.**

6 Unscramble the anagrams to find:

a	a day of the week	NAMOCEDI
b	something you buy in the **farmacia**	TIOCRTE
c	a place to live	LLAVI
d	a vegetable	TATAPA

7 Which one would you use . . .

a   . . . when someone's speaking too quickly?
b   . . . to explain you're not from the area?
c   . . . if you don't know something?
d   . . . to find out how to say something in Italian?
e   . . . when you'd like to hear something again?
f   . . . to say you're sorry?

8 Make the connection – match a word from A with one from B.

A	B
formaggio	**casa**
lire	**lavoro**
piscina	**giornale**
ristorante	**pizza**
francobollo	**acqua**
appartamento	**banca**
edicola	**trattoria**
professione	**cartolina**

9 Fill the gaps with **questo**, **questa**, **questi** or **queste**.

a   **Mi dà mezzo chilo di** .... **funghi.**
b   **Quanto costa** .... **cartolina?**
c   **Vorrei due bottiglie di** .... **vino rosso.**
d   **Quanto costano** .... **pesche?**
e   **È aperto** .... **ristorante?**
f   **Prendo duecentocinquanta grammi di** .... **fragole.**

10 Read Chris's postcard to Elena and decide whether the statements which follow are **vero** or **falso**.

Cara Elena,

Sono qui vicino a Rapallo in vacanza! L'albergo ha una piscina e un campo da tennis, e ci sono negozi, teatri, cinema e musei in centro città (non è lontano e c'è l'autobus).

Stefano arriva venerdì – lavora in un negozio da lunedì a giovedì. Sabato andiamo a Firenze.

Saluti Chris

Sig.ra ROSSI Elena
Via Michelangelo, 20
41101 MODENA

		vero	falso
a	Chris lavora a Rapallo.		
b	L'albergo è in centro.		
c	C'è una piscina all'albergo.		
d	Elena arriva venerdì.		
e	Stefano lavora mercoledì.		
f	Elena abita a Modena.		
g	Stefano è studente all'università.		

11 Practise answering aloud the following questions about yourself. Why not record an 'interview' with yourself on cassette?

Come ti chiami?
Dove abiti?
Lavori? Che lavoro fai? Dove lavori? Lavori ogni giorno?
Sei inglese? Di dove sei?
Qual è il tuo numero di telefono?
Parli francese . . . tedesco . . . italiano . . . inglese?

8 OTTO

Vorrei una camera

- checking in at reception
- finding a hotel room
- booking ahead by phone
- making requests

In Italia . . .

there is a wide choice of accommodation, ranging from the basic **pensione** (guesthouse) or one-star hotel to the five-star **categoria lusso** (luxury) hotel.

The best place for advice and information is the **azienda di turismo** who will supply lists of places to stay and often will ring to check availability and even make reservations. The price of **una camera** (a hotel room) is on display in the room, usually on the back of the door. This price is quoted **tutto incluso** (all inclusive) which means that it includes tax and service charges but not **la prima colazione** (breakfast). Many people opt to have breakfast in a bar.

Checking in at reception

1 Listen to these key phrases.

Ho prenotato . . .	I've booked . . .
una camera singola	
una camera doppia . . .	
a due letti	
matrimoniale	
con bagno	
con doccia	
al terzo piano	on the third floor
al secondo/primo piano	on the second/first floor
al pianterreno	on the ground floor
Il suo nome?	Your name?
Il suo passaporto, per favore	Your passport, please

2 Maria Cavalleri is in reception at the Albergo Giotto. Listen as she
greets the guests and checks their name in the register before giving
them their key (**la chiave**).
Listen several times, then fill in the details missing from the grid below.

	sing dopp./mat. dopp./2 letti	bagno doccia	numero della camera	piano
sig. Pittara	....	....	....	....
sig.ra Rossini	....	....	....	....
sig. Barucci	....	....	....	....

3 Listen again and make a note of where **l'ascensore** (the lift) is.

....

Finding a hotel room

I   Listen to these key phrases.

Vorrei una camera	I'd like a room
. . . per stasera	. . . for tonight
. . . per tre notti	. . . for three nights
. . . per una settimana	. . . for a week
fino a . . .	until . . .
Come si scrive?	How do you spell it?

2   Two men arrive at the hotel reception without reservations. What does Maria say to check that the first man wants a room for tonight only? How long does the second man want to stay?

3   Listen to Alberto saying the Italian alphabet and then spelling out his own name. What is his **cognome**?

A B C D E F G H I L M N O P Q R S T U V Z

In italiano . . .

j (i lunga), k (cappa), w (doppia vu), x (ics) and **y (ipsilon)** are not in the Italian alphabet but are used to spell foreign words.

4   Now listen to the whole of the conversation between Maria and the two men and note down their names.

a ....   *b* ....

5   Now practise spelling your own name in Italian.

6   How would you say you'd like the following?

- for tonight
- for 3 nights
- for a week
- until Sunday

Booking ahead by phone

1   Listen to these key phrases.

Pronto	Hello (on the telephone)
Un attimo	One moment
Vorrei prenotare una camera	I'd like to book a room
Per quando?	When for?
Siamo al completo	We're full

gennaio January	**febbraio** February	**marzo** March	**aprile** April
maggio May	**giugno** June	**luglio** July	**agosto** August
settembre September	**ottobre** October	**novembre** November	**dicembre** December

In italiano . . .

dates are expressed with the number (two, eleven, twenty-seven, etc.) and the month. They start with **il**:

il quindici giugno	15th June
il ventisette agosto	27th August
fino al dodici maggio	until 12th May
dal 30 luglio al 6 agosto	from 30th July to 6th August

The only exception is the first of the month, which is **il primo**:

il primo marzo	1st March

2   The receptionist is taking three bookings over the phone. Can you work out the dates these people want rooms for?

a ....   *b* ....   *c* ....

Making requests

1 Listen to these key phrases.

Posso . . . /Possiamo . . .   Can I . . . /Can we . . .
. . . vedere la camera?   . . . see the room?
. . . pagare con la carta di credito? . . . pay by credit card?
. . . lasciare la valigia qui?   . . . leave the suitcase here?
. . . telefonare da qui?   . . . telephone from here?
. . . parcheggiare qui?   . . . park here?

2 Some of the guests are leaving while others are arriving, and each one asks the receptionist if they can do something.
As you listen, can you work out who wants to do what?

signor Belloni   leave a suitcase in the hotel
Lorna Tonino   make a telephone call
Luigi Ciani   pay by credit card
signor Chini   speak to the manager
                         see the room on offer

3 A couple arriving at the hotel are unsure where to leave their car. Listen to their conversation and decide:

- where they are advised to park
- what their **targa** (car registration number) is

P

Parcheggio

Put it all together

1 Match the Italian with the English.

a	**Vorrei prenotare . . .**	Can I . . . ?
b	**Ho prenotato . . .**	I'd like to book . . .
c	**Avete . . . ?**	I've booked . . .
d	**Posso . . . ?**	Hello
e	**Possiamo . . . ?**	Have you got . . . ?
f	**Pronto**	Can we . . . ?

2 Complete the following:

a **Ho prenotato** ....

b **Vorrei** ....

c **Avete** .... ?

d **Ha** .... ? (1 notte)

e **Vorrei prenotare** .... (21 marzo)

f **Posso** .... ?

Hotel Astoria ★★★★
Via Aquila Nera, 22 Tel: 035/938045
- 28 camere con servizi privati, aria condizionata, TV
- parcheggio privato
- vicino al centro storico
- chiuso 30 novembre–1 marzo

3 If you asked the proprietors of the Hotel Astoria the following
questions, would they answer **sì** or **no**?

		Sì	No
a	**C'è un ristorante?**		
b	**Possiamo parcheggiare?**		
c	**Avete una piscina?**		
d	**L'albergo è lontano dal centro città?**		
e	**È aperto in gennaio?**		

Now you're talking!

1   Take the part of Anna Mannoni arriving at the Hotel Giotto.

◇ **Buongiorno, signora. Mi dica.**
◆ Ask if they have a room.
◇ **Singola o doppia?**
◆ Say single, with bathroom.
◇ **Per quante notti?**
◆ Say for tonight.
◇ **Va bene, signora – camera numero 245 al secondo piano.**
◆ Ask if you can see the room.
◇ **Certo, signora.**

2   Now take the part of John Graham.

◆ Greet the receptionist and say you've booked a room.
◇ **Il suo nome, signore?**
◆ Tell her who you are.
◇ **Allora, una camera doppia con bagno.**
◆ This isn't what you booked. Say no, a single room with bath.
◇ **. . . per tre notti?**
◆ Say no, for two nights – until 22nd August.
◇ **Che strano. Come si scrive il suo nome?**
◆ Spell out Graham.
◇ **Ah signore – sì, scusi – camera singola per due notti.**
◆ Ask if you can pay by credit card.
◇ **Sì, certo.**

Quiz

1 Name two things in a hotel beginning with **c**.

c................ c................

2 Which month follows **luglio**?

3 Which date is **il primo maggio**?

4 What is **il primo piano**?

5 What is **la prima colazione**?

6 If someone asked you for your **targa**, what information would you give them?

7 When would you use **posso** and when **possiamo**?

8 If you were quoted a price **tutto incluso** in a hotel, would you assume breakfast was included?

Now check whether you can . . .

☐ say you've booked a room

☐ ask for a room in a hotel and specify single or double

☐ say whether you want a room with or without a bath or shower

☐ say how long you want the room for and specify dates

☐ ask to see the room

☐ ask if you can pay by credit card

☐ spell your name in Italian

If you travel to Italy with someone else you might prefer to say 'we . . .' rather than 'I . . .'. For nearly all verbs, this involves substituting the **-o** ending with **-iamo**:

posso   **possiamo**
abito (I live)   **abitiamo** (we live).

There are a few exceptions, of course. Look out for **siamo** (we are) and **abbiamo** (we have).

A che ora parte?

- asking about public transport
- finding out train times
- buying tickets
- checking travel details

In Italia . . .

public transport is generally cheap and reliable and an excellent way to see the country. There are **treni** (trains), **pullman** (coaches) and, to and from the many Italian islands, **traghetti** (ferries) and **aliscafi** (hydrofoils).

In town, **autobus** (buses) are cheap and frequent and some towns also have a tram system. **Roma**, **Milano** and **Napoli** have a **metro** (underground).

To travel on a **rapido** – the **Intercity** and **Pendolino**, fast trains which link the major cities – you have to pay a **supplemento** and book in advance (**prenotare**).

Asking about public transport

1 Listen to these key phrases.

C'è un autobus per . . . ?	Is there a bus to . . . ?
C'è un pullman per . . . ?	Is there a coach to . . . ?
Quando parte?	When does it leave?
Ce n'è uno . . .	There's one . . .
. . . alle dieci	. . . at 10 o'clock
. . . ogni ora	. . . every hour
. . . ogni mezz'ora	. . . every half hour

to say what time something takes place, the key word is **alle:**

alle due `02:00`   **alle dieci** `10:00`   **alle diciannove** `19:00`

The 24-hour clock is universally used with travel times.

2 Listen to three queries at the **ufficio informazioni** (information office) and tick the frequency of the services and the next departure times. The first one has been done for you.

	Ce n'è uno ogni . . .			Parte alle . . .		
	¹/₂ ora	ora	2 ore	7.00	10.00	11.00
L'autobus per la stazione	✔				✔	
L'autobus per piazza Garibaldi						
Il pullman per l'aeroporto						

3 How would you ask if there is:

- a coach to the airport?
- a bus to the station?
- one at 10 o'clock?

Finding out train times

| Listen to these key phrases.

A che ora . . .	What time . . .
parte il prossimo treno . . .	does the next train leave . . .
. . . per Roma?	. . . for Rome?
A che ora . . .	What time . . .
arriva il treno . . .	does the train arrive . . .
. . . a Roma?	. . . in Rome?
. . . da Roma?	. . . from Rome?

In italiano . . .

hours are separated from minutes by **e** (and):
alle nove e venti   at 09.20
alle quattordici e cinquantadue   at 14.52

2   Listen to people enquiring about trains to various cities and fill in the missing departure and arrival times.

PARTENZE (departures)   **ARRIVI** (arrivals)

Roma ....   **Venezia** ....
Bologna ....   **Padova** ....
Bergamo ....

3   Listen again and decide **vero** or **falso** for the following:

	vero	falso
a **C'è un treno per Bologna ogni ora.**		
b **Il treno arriva a Bergamo alle 10.55.**		

4   How would you ask what time:

- the next train leaves for Florence?
- it arrives in Florence?
- the train arrives from Venice?

Buying tickets . . .

1 Listen to these key phrases.

Un biglietto per . . .	A ticket for . . .
Un biglietto per . . .	A ticket for . . .
andata . . .	single . . .
. . . o andata e ritorno?	. . . or return?
prima classe	first class
seconda classe	second class
con supplemento	with a supplement
Da che binario parte?	Which platform does it leave from?

2 Listen to several people buying train tickets and indicate in the grid
what kind of ticket they buy.

	Biglietto		Classe		Supplemento	
	andata	andata e ritorno	1a	2a	Sì	No
Bologna						
Milano						
Verona						
Firenze						
Roma						

3 Listen again to the last recording. The **bigliettaio** (ticket clerk) tells
two of the people buying tickets which platform their trains will leave
from. Make a note of their destinations and the platform numbers.

	Treno per . . .	Binario numero . . .
a	....	....
b	....	....

. . . and checking travel details

4 Listen to these key phrases.

È diretto?	Is it a through train?
Devo . . . ?	Do I have to . . . ?
Deve . . .	You have to . . .
. . . cambiare	. . . change
. . . andare	. . . go
. . . prenotare il posto	. . . make a seat reservation
. . . scendere	. . . get off (a train or bus)
Non capisco	I don't understand

5 Listen as passengers check the details of their journey in the **ufficio informazioni** and tick the correct information. The first is travelling to **Napoli**.

Deve cambiare?   **Sì**   **No**

6 The next passenger, travelling to Arezzo, has difficulty with the information he's being given. He speaks English – can you act as interpreter and tell him:

- what time his train leaves?
- whether he has to change?
- the cost of the ticket?
- any other information he needs to know?

7 Listen as Mario is given some information about bus tickets and bus stops (**fermate**), and then fill the gaps with **devo** or **deve**.

Mario	**Dove posso comprare un biglietto per l'autobus?**
signora	.... **andare in tabaccheria – ce n'è una lì, a destra.**
Mario	**Grazie.**
Mario	**Scusi,** .... **scendere qui per il Duomo?**
signora 2	**No – alla prossima fermata.**
Mario	**Grazie.**

Put it all together

1   Select the answer for each question.

    a   **C'è un treno diretto per Napoli?**
    b   **A che ora parte il prossimo treno per Padova?**
    c   **A che ora arriva questo treno a Chiusi?**
    d   **Devo prenotare il posto?**
    e   **C'è un pullman per Verona?**
    f   **Dove posso comprare i biglietti per l'autobus?**

        1   **In edicola o in tabaccheria.**
        2   **No, deve cambiare a Roma.**
        3   **Sì, deve prenotare per l'Intercity.**
        4   **Ce n'è uno ogni due ore e mezza.**
        5   **Parte alle nove e venticinque.**
        6   **Alle quindici e dodici.**

2   Work out how you would say the following in Italian, using the 24-hour clock:

    a   at 7 a.m.   *d*   at 11 p.m.
    b   at 7 p.m.   *e*   at 8.25 a.m.
    c   at 11 a.m.   *f*   at 8.25 p.m.

3   Choose the correct ending for each sentence.

    a   **Mi dà un biglietto di**   **venti minuti.**
    b   **C'è un autobus ogni**   **nove e venti.**
    c   **Deve scendere alla**   **ventidue euro.**
    d   **Il prossimo treno parte alle**   **seconda classe.**
    e   **Il biglietto costa**   **seconda fermata.**

4   How would you finish the question: **Devo** .... **?**

    a   to find out if you have to change
    b   to ask if a seat reservation is necessary
    c   if you have to get off the bus here

Now you're talking!

1   Imagine you're staying in Umbria and want to see the area using public
    transport. First, to the coach station.

 ◆ Ask the lady in the office if there's a coach to Perugia.
 ◇ **Ce n'è uno ogni due ore.**
 ◆ Ask what time the next coach leaves.
 ◇ **Alle dieci.**
 ◆ Find out if you have to make a seat reservation.
 ◇ **No, non è necessario.**
 ◆ Ask how much the ticket costs.
 ◇ **Andata o andata e ritorno?**
 ◆ Say a return.
 ◇ **Quattordici euro.**

2   Next, to Orvieto by train.

 ◆ Ask the man in the ticket office what time the next train leaves for
   Orvieto.
 ◇ **Orvieto . . . alle nove e quaranta.**
 ◆ Find out what time it arrives in Orvieto.
 ◇ **Alle dieci e quarantasette.**
 ◆ Ask if you have to change.
 ◇ **No, è diretto.**
 ◆ Say you'd like a return ticket.
 ◇ **Prima o seconda classe?**
 ◆ Say second class, then ask which platform the train leaves from.
 ◇ **Binario numero quattro.**
 ◆ Thank him.

3   Finally, by bus to the town centre. You meet a lady at the bus stop.
    You want to ask her the following:

 ◆ the time of the next bus
 ◆ if there's a **tabaccheria** nearby

Quiz

1   To say 'every ten minutes', what word will you need to add?
    .... **dieci minuti.**
2   How do you say you don't understand?
3   What's special about the **Pendolino** and the **Intercity**?
4   If someone starts their sentence to you with **Deve**, what are they telling you?
5   What time does something start if it starts **alle diciotto**?
6   Is **un biglietto di andata e ritorno** a single or a return ticket?
7   What are the words to look out for if you want a non-smoking carriage?
8   If you hear an announcement about **il treno da Roma**, is it about the train from Rome or to Rome?

Now check whether you can . . .

☐   ask if there's a bus or a coach going to a particular place

☐   find out when it leaves

☐   ask what time trains (or other means of transport) depart and arrive

☐   find out what platform a train leaves from

☐   find out whether you have to make a seat reservation

☐   ask for a single or return ticket

☐   find out whether you have to pay a supplement

☐   ask if you have to change

☐   say you don't understand

When learning a language, it can be very easy to underestimate how much you know. Go back occasionally to one of the early units to prove to yourself how much you've learnt. Think also about what you find easy . . . and difficult. If you can identify your strengths and weaknesses, you can build on your strengths and find ways of compensating for the weaknesses.

Buon appetito!

- reading the menu
- asking about items on the menu
- ordering a meal
- saying what you like and don't like
- paying compliments

In Italia . . .

the best place to eat is the one full of local people, away from the main tourist spots. You can generally eat just as well in a small, family-run **trattoria** as in a smart **ristorante** – and pay a lot less.

Italian cooking makes use of fresh local produce and varies greatly from region to region. Look out for the words **specialità della regione** (local speciality) and **cucina casalinga** or **cucina casareccia** (home cooking).

Il pranzo is the main meal of the day, served between midday and around 2.30 p.m. **La cena**, the evening meal, is served from around 8 p.m.

At the start of a meal, it is customary to wish people **Buon appetito!** (Enjoy your meal!).

Antipasti
Antipasto della casa

> Starters, usually cold meats, sea food, olives and various vegetables.

Primi (piatti)
Zuppa del giorno
Minestrone
Tagliatelle al ragù / al pomodoro
Cannelloni al forno
Risotto alla marinara

> First courses, usually soup, pasta or risotto

Secondi (piatti)
Bistecca alla griglia
Filetto di maiale ai funghi
Agnello arrosto
Petto di pollo all'aglio
Pesce del giorno

> Second courses, usually **carne** (meat), **pesce** (fish) or poultry

Contorni
Zucchini, Spinaci, Carote, Broccoli
Patate ~ fritte o arroste
Insalata ~ verde o mista

> Side dishes of vegetables or salad

Dessert
Frutta di stagione
Gelati assortiti
Sorbetto alla fragola
Torta della casa
Tiramisù
Formaggi assortiti della regione

> Also referred to as **dolci**

pane e coperto

> Bread and cover charge

Reading the menu

1 Read the menu opposite and see how much of it you already understand or can guess.

2 Now read through the following notes, then go back and read the menu again. You may also need to consult the glossary.

Some of the terms you find in a menu are very general.

. . . del giorno	. . . of the day
. . . della casa	the house . . .
. . . della regione	local . . .
. . . di stagione	. . . in season
. . . misto	mixed . . .
. . . assortiti	an assortment of . . .

Others, starting with **al**, **alla**, **all'**, **alle**, **ai** or **agli**, are more precise and refer to the main ingredient of a dish, the way it is cooked or to a particular tradition.

al pomodoro with tomato	**alla griglia** grilled
all'aglio with garlic	**ai ferri** barbecued
ai funghi with mushrooms	**al forno** baked
alla marinara with seafood	**allo spiedo** on a spit
al ragù with bolognese sauce	**alla romana** Roman style

Fish is usually fresh and often referred to on the menu simply as **pesce del giorno**.

Meat is usually **manzo** (beef), **agnello** (lamb), **vitello** (veal) or **pollo** (chicken) but you can also find **coniglio** (rabbit), **capretto** (goat) and **cinghiale** (wild boar). It can be served as described above, or possibly

arrosto roasted	**fritto** fried
in umido stewed	**bollito, lesso** boiled

Asking about items on the menu

1 Listen to these key phrases.

Cos'è . . . ?   What is . . . ?
Com'è . . . ?   What's . . . like?
Come sono . . . ?   What are . . . like?

2 In the Trattoria Chiezzi, Emilio the waiter shows some people to their table (**tavolo**). How many of them are there? What do they order as an **aperitivo**?

3 Emilio tells them what there is for the **primo piatto**. Some of the items are on the menu on page 88. As you hear these, put a tick by them.

4 Listen as they ask Emilio some questions about the dishes. What is the soup of the day? Can you identify two ingredients missing from this recipe for **spaghetti alla carbonara**?

Spaghetti alla carbonara
Ingredienti:

spaghetti
uova (eggs)
....
panna (cream)
....
pepe (pepper)

In italiano . . .

because pasta dishes are plural – **i cannelloni**, **gli spaghetti**, **le tagliatelle**, **le lasagne**, etc. – you say **come sono?** not **com'è?** to ask what a pasta dish is like.

5 How would you ask what the following are like?

• risotto
• ravioli

Ordering a meal

1 Listen to these key phrases.

Pronto/a/i/e per ordinare?	Ready to order?
Cosa prende/prendono?	What will you have?
Cosa consiglia?	What do you recommend?
Da bere?	To drink?
Prendo . . .	I'll have . . .
Niente . . . per me	No . . . for me

2 A couple with their daughter order their **primo piatto**.
Listen and complete this part of their conversation.

signore .... **il minestrone.**
signora **Io** .... **il risotto ai funghi, e le
tagliatelle al ragù** .... **mia figlia.**

3 A woman eating alone at the next table skips the **primo**. Listen to her
ordering a **secondo piatto** and a **contorno** and tick what she
chooses from this menu.

Primi	zuppa di verdura
	lasagne al forno
Secondi	pesce del giorno
	filetto di maiale
	agnello arrosto con aglio e rosmarino
Contorni	broccoli, piselli, zucchini, patate, insalata

4 Listen as she orders something to drink.
Does she want sparkling or still water?
Does she order red or white wine?
Does she have ¹/₂ litre or ¹/₄ litre?

5 How would you say you'll have the fish and a salad?

Saying what you like and don't like . . .

1   Listen to these key phrases.

Vorrei assaggiare . . .	I'd like to taste . . .
Mi piace . . .	I like . . .
Non mi piace . . .	I don't like . . .
Le piace . . . ?	Do you like . . . ? **(lei)**
Ti piace . . . ?	Do you like . . . ? **(tu)**
È buono/buonissimo	It's good/extremely good

2   One table has finished their **secondo**. Listen as the man calls Emilio over. What does he say to attract Emilio's attention?
Tick which of the following they are offered for dessert.

mele	**melone**	**fragole**
formaggio	**gelato**	**yogurt**
torta di mele	**torta al cioccolato**	**tiramisù**

3   Listen as Emilio brings the desserts over and decide who likes and who doesn't like the **dolcelatte** – a local cheese.

<table>
<tr><td></td><td align="center">mi piace</td><td align="center">non mi piace</td></tr>
<tr><td>signora 1</td><td rowspan="3"></td><td rowspan="3"></td></tr>
<tr><td>signore 1</td></tr>
<tr><td>signora 2</td></tr>
</table>

In italiano . . .

to say something is extremely . . . or very . . . , you can add **-issimo** to the adjective minus its final vowel.

il formaggio è buon<u>o</u>	**buonissim<u>o</u>**
la torta è buon<u>a</u>	**buonissim<u>a</u>**
i gelati sono buon<u>i</u>	**buonissim<u>i</u>**
le fragole sono buon<u>e</u>	**buonissim<u>e</u>**

4   How would you say you like . . .   ● white wine?   ● cheese?

. . . and paying compliments

5 Listen to these key phrases.

Tutto bene?	Is everything all right?
Complimenti	Congratulations
È delizioso!	It's delicious!
Le piacciono . . .	Do you like . . .
. . . i formaggi italiani?	. . . Italian cheeses?
Mi piacciono . . .	I like . . .
. . . tutti i formaggi	. . . all cheeses

6 The **padrone** (owner) of the Trattoria Chiezzi comes into the dining room to ask if everything is all right. Tick any of the following which you hear.

Complimenti!   mi piacciono   è buonissimo   è deliziosa

è molto buono   Che buono!   è delizioso

In italiano . . .

to talk about liking something which is plural, you replace **piace** with **piacciono**:

Le piacciono i cannelloni?	Do you like cannelloni?
Sì, mi piacciono	Yes, I like them
Ti piacciono le cipolle?	Do you like onions?
No, non mi piacciono molto	No, I don't like them much

7 The family is ready for dessert. What do they all (**tutti**) choose?

8 How would you say you like . . .

● strawberries?   ● apples?

Put it all together

1 Match the Italian with the English.

a	**della casa**	baked
b	**alla griglia**	with tomatoes
c	**fritto**	of the day
d	**di stagione**	of the house
e	**del giorno**	in season
f	**al forno**	grilled
g	**al pomodoro**	fried

2 Put the following dishes in the right columns.

patate, coniglio, gelato, risotto, ravioli, vitello, insalata, sorbetto, agnello, zuppa, torta, zucchini

primi piatti	secondi piatti	contorni	dolci

3 How would you say you like the following?

a	**il prosciutto**	b	**le tagliatelle al ragù**
c	**il risotto alla marinara**	d	**il vitello ai funghi**
e	**la torta di mele**	f	**le fragole**

How would you say you don't like them?

4 Can you supply the final vowel to the adjectives in these sentences? **Ottimo** and **squisito** are often used to describe something which is excellent.

a **Questo vino è ottim_.**
b **Gli spaghetti sono buonissim_.**
c **Complimenti per una cena squisit_.**
d **Le fragole sono molto buon_.**
e **Questa torta è delizios_.**

Now you're talking!

I   Imagine you are going for a meal in the Trattoria Chiezzi with a partner who doesn't speak Italian. You might need the menu from page 88.

You're greeted by Emilio . . .
◇ **Buongiorno, signori. Tavolo per due?**
◈ Say yes, for two.
◇ **Ecco il menù.**
◈ Thank him.

He returns a few minutes later.
◇ **Pronti per ordinare?**
◈ Ask for seafood risotto and cannelloni.
◇ **E per secondo?**
◈ Ask what he recommends.
◇ **Il pesce è buono oggi – molto buono.**
◈ Order the fish and the chicken in garlic.
◇ **E come contorno?**
◈ Order potatoes and courgettes.

When he brings the food . . .
◇ **Ecco . . . pesce . . . e pollo. Buon appetito.**
◈ Say you'd like a carafe of red wine.
◇ **Un litro?**
◈ Say half a litre.

He comes back when you have finished.
◇ **Tutto bene? Le piace il pesce?**
◈ Say yes, you like it, it's very good.
◇ **Dessert, signori?**
◈ Ask what the **torta della casa** is.
◇ **È una torta di pere con panna. Le piacciono le pere?**
◈ Say you like them a lot but you don't like cream.
◈ Order ice cream and cheese.
◇ **Va bene.**

Quiz

1. How would you ask for a table for two?
2. What is the main ingredient of a dish **all'aglio**?
3. To say you like **lasagne al forno** would you use **mi piace** or **mi piacciono**?
4. How do you say you don't want a pudding?
5. What do you say to attract the waiter's attention?
6. Is lamb **vitello** or **agnello**?
7. What is the word for 'very good indeed' when talking about **il tiramisù**?
8. Which one of these is not a **contorno**?
   spinaci; **insalata**; **maiale**; **zucchini**
9. Before starting your meal, what would you say to the people eating with you?

Now check whether you can . . .

   ■ understand the main points of an Italian menu

   ■ ask about items on the menu

   ■ order a meal with drinks

   ■ say what you like and what you don't like

   ■ ask others what they like

   ■ pay a compliment

Bravo! You have reached the end of *Talk Italian*.

And now . . . prepare yourself for the **Controllo finale** (final checkpoint) with some revision. Listen to the conversations again – the more you listen the more confident you will become. You can test your knowledge of the key phrases by covering up the English on the lists. Look back at the final pages of each unit and use the quizzes and checklists to assess how much you remember.

Take every opportunity to speak Italian; if no one else is available, talk aloud to yourself!

Controllo finale

Imagine you have just arrived in Italy on holiday . . .

1 It's Sunday. You arrive at Santa Maria Novella station in Florence, tired and thirsty, and look for a bar. Which of these questions would you ask?

   a **Scusi, dov'è il duomo?**
   b **Scusi, c'è un albergo qui?**
   c **Scusi, c'è un bar qui vicino?**

2 Having found one, you go to the **cassa**. Now listen to the audio and be ready to order a drink.

You	....
Cassiera	**Un euro e ottantadue. Ecco lo scontrino.**
You	....

   a How much change should you expect from a 10 euro note?
   b What is a **scontrino**?

3 After your drink, how would you ask the barman . . .

   a if you can make a phone call from here?
   b where the toilet is?
   c if the tourist office is open today?
   d how much the postcards cost?

Scusi, signore

4 You then ask him where the Hotel Arcangelo is. Listen and make a note in English of the directions he gives you.

....

....

....

5 Before finding the hotel, you go back to the station to find out when the first train leaves for Rome on Tuesday morning, what time it arrives and how much a single ticket costs.

For each question, choose the correct option.

a **A che ora parte il <u>primo</u> / <u>prossimo</u> treno per Roma <u>martedì</u> / <u>mercoledì</u>?**

b **A che ora arriva <u>da</u> / <u>a</u> Roma?**

c **Quanto <u>costa</u> / <u>costano</u> un biglietto <u>di andata e ritorno</u> / <u>di andata</u>?**

6 At the Arcangelo you have already booked a single room with shower until Tuesday. At reception, after saying who you are, which of the following would you say?

a **Vorrei una camera singola con bagno fino a giovedì.**

b **Ho prenotato una camera singola senza bagno fino a martedì.**

c **Avete una camera a due letti fino a mercoledì?**

d **Ho prenotato una camera singola con doccia fino a martedì.**

7 Listen to the receptionist's reply. Make a note in English of the two things she asks you, and also of your room number and which floor it's on.

a ....

b ....

c **Camera** ....   **Piano** ....

8 The Hotel Arcangelo will change money for you. Listen to the manager telling you the rate of exchange (**il cambio**) for the pound (**sterlina**). What does he say is the current rate?

a € 1,56

b € 1,66

c € 1,76

9 That evening in the hotel bar, you start chatting to Paul Durand who is French from **Nizza** (Nice). He's in marketing and travels a lot. Listen to his plans for the week and note where he is going in the diary. **Vado** means 'I'm going'.

Monday	Thursday
Tuesday	Friday
Wednesday	Saturday
	Sunday

10 Can you now work out how Paul would answer these three questions?

a **Come si chiama?**
b **È italiano?**
c **Dove abita?**

What questions would you need to ask him if these are his answers?

d ....
Si, sono sposato.

e ....
Si chiama Christiane.

f ....
Sì, ho una figlia – Amélie.

g ....
Ha sei anni.

h ....
Sono direttore del marketing.

i ....
Sì, parlo inglese . . . e anche italiano, tedesco e giapponese.

j ....
No, non mi piace lo sport.

Finally, he asks you some questions. Listen to the audio.

11 Paul is planning to bring his family to Italy on a camping holiday and shows you information about Campeggio La Pineta.

★★★★ Campeggio La Pineta
Tel: 059/22339

	alta stagione luglio/agosto	bassa stagione aprile – giugno settembre/ottobre
piazzola	€21	€17
adulto	€15	€10
bambino (2 – 12)	€6,50	€4,50

Prices are per night. Can you work out the price for Paul and his family to stay in La Pineta for six nights in July? **Una piazzola** is a place in a campsite. If he pays by cheque, how will he write the amount in words?

12 The two of you decide not to eat in the hotel but to try this restaurant Paul has seen advertised.

ristorante
AL VIGNETO
specialità carne e pesce alla griglia
cucina casareccia tradizionale • vini locali
posizione panoramica con giardino

chiuso il lunedì da novembre a aprile

a What is the house speciality?
b Is the restaurant closed tonight (Sunday)?
c What kind of wines can you expect?
d What is special about **cucina casareccia**?

Audio scripts and answers

This section contains scripts of all the conversations. Answers which consist of words and phrases from the conversations are given in bold type in the scripts. Other answers are given separately.

Unit I **Buongiorno!**

Pages 8 & 9 **Saying hello and goodbye**

2 • Buongiorno, **signore**. *(m.)*
  • Buongiorno, signora.
  • Ah, **signora Riccardi** – buongiorno.
  • Come sta?
  • Bene grazie.
  • Buongiorno!
  • Buongiorno, **signor Chiesa**.
  The first person is a man.

3 • **Buona sera**.
  • Buona sera, signor Conti.
  • Buona sera, signora. Come sta?
  • Bene, grazie. E lei?
  • Bene, grazie.

4 • **Ciao**, Carla, **buongiorno**.
  • **Ciao**, Giorgio.
  • **Ciao**! Come stai?
  • Bene, grazie.
  • **Ciao, buongiorno**.

6 • Arrivederci, Claudia, **buongiorno**.
  • Arrivederci, signor Chiesa.
  • Arrivederci, signora.
  • Arrivederci, signor Conti.

7 • **Ciao**, Angela. **Arrivederci**.
  • **Ciao**, Francesca. **Buongiorno**.

8 • Buona notte, **signore**. *(m.)*
  • Buona notte, **signora**. *(f.)*
  • Buona notte, **signora Ricci**. *(f.)*
  • Buona notte, **signor Conti**. *(m.)*
  Two men and two women.

9 • Buongiorno, signor Calvi.
  • Ciao, Carlo, buona sera.
  • Buona sera, signore.
  • Buona sera, signora.
  • Ciao, Lucia.

10 • Come sta, signor Calvi?
  • Come stai, Carlo?
  • Arrivederci, signor Calvi.

Pages 10 & 11 **Introducing yourself and getting to know people**

2 • Buongiorno, signora. Sono **Enrico Piacenza**.
  • Buongiorno. Sono **Giovanna Ricci**.
  • Signora Ricci . . . buongiorno.
  • Io sono **Roberto Riccardi**.
  Roberto (not Paolo) Riccardi.

3 • Buongiorno, signore. Signore, **lei è**?
  • Mancini. Sono Luciano Mancini.

5 • **Mi chiama** Francesca Como. **Come si chiama?**
  • Luciano, Luciano Mancini. **Piacere.**
  • **Piacere.**

6 • Buona sera, signora. Enrico Piacenza.
  • Piacere. Io mi chiamo Giovanna Ricci.
  • **Scusi?**
  • Ricci – Giovanna Ricci.
  • Piacere.

7 • Buongiorno. Come si **chiama**?
  • **Mi** chiamo Franco Lelli.
  • Ciao. **Come** ti chiami?
  • **Mi** chiamo Giulia.
  • E tu, come ti chiami?
  • Mi **chiamo** Marcella.

8 • Ciao **Gemma**. Ciao **Guido**.
• **Giovanna**! Ciao! Come stai?
• Buona sera. Come stai?
• Bene, bene . . . questo è **Geraldo**.

Page 12 Put it all together

1 *a* Buona notte; *b* Ciao; *c* Mi chiamo;
d Io sono; *e* Buongiorno; *f* Come sta?;
g Arrivederci; *h* Buona sera;
i Come si chiama?; *j* Piacere.

2 *a* Buongiorno, signora. – Buongiorno,
signore.
b Buona sera – Ciao, buona sera.
c Ciao, come stai? – Bene.
d Buona notte. – Buona notte.

Page 13 Now you're talking!

1 • Buongiorno. Come sta?
• **Bene grazie, e lei?**
• Bene, grazie.
• **Buongiorno, signora. Sono
+ *your name.***
• Piacere. Io sono Anna Alberti.
• **Scusi?**
• Anna Alberti.
• **Piacere.**

• **Buongiorno. Lei è Luciano
Mironi?**
• No, sono Luciano Mancini.
• **Io sono + *your name*. Piacere.**
• Piacere.
• **Arrivederci, Anna, arrivederci
Luciano.**
• Arrivederci.

2 • **Buona sera, signora.**
• Buona sera. Come sta?
• **Bene, grazie . . . Ciao!**
• Buona sera.
• **Come ti chiami?**
• Mi chiamo Giulia.
• **E come stai, Giulia?**
• Bene, grazie.
• **Arrivederci, buona sera.**

Page 14 Quiz

1 to say hello or goodbye informally;
2 Piacere; *3* late afternoon and evening;
4 lei; *5* before a surname; *6* Bene, grazie –
e lei? 7 to wish someone good night;
8 io sono / mi chiamo; *9* Moschino;
10 Come ti chiami?

Unit 2 Di dov'è?

**Pages 16 & 17 Talking about where
you're from and your nationality**

2 • Signora, lei è inglese?
• Sì, sono **inglese**.
• Lei è inglese?
• No. Io sono **americano**. Sono di
Chicago.
• Buongiorno, signore. Lei è
americano?
• No, io non sono americano, sono
inglese.
• E lei, signora? È inglese o americana?
• Sono **australiana**!
• Di dov'è?
• Sono di Perth.

3 • Come ti chiami?
• Fiorella.
• Sei italiana, no?
• Sì.
• **Di dove sei?**
• Di **Bergamo**.

4
Italia	**italiano**
Inghilterra	**inglese**
Scozia	**scozzese**
Irlanda	**irlandese**
Galles	**gallese**
Stati Uniti	**americano**
Australia	**australiano**
Svizzera	**svizzero**
Francia	**francese**
Germania	**tedesco**
Spagna	**spagnolo**
Canadà	**canadese**

6
- Antonio è **spagnolo**, di Madrid.
- Helen è **americana**.
- Mike è di Toronto, è **canadese**.
- Anna è **scozzese**. È di Edimburgo.

Page 18 Saying what you do for a living

2
- Signore, che lavoro fa?
- Sono **giornalista**.
- Che lavoro fa?
- Sono **ingegnere**.
- Signora, che lavoro fa?
- Sono **segretaria**.

3
- Che lavoro fa?
- Sono **guida**.
- Tu sei studente?
- No, non sono studente.
- Che lavoro fai?
- Sono **ragioniere**.
- Lei è artista?
- Sì, ma sono **disoccupato**.

ma = *but*

4
- Buongiorno, signore.
- Che lavoro fa lei?
- Sono **professore d'italiano** *(teacher of Italian)*.
- Lei è italiano, vero?
- No, non sono italiano – sono **scozzese** (Scottish).

Page 19 Giving your phone number

2
- Qual è il tuo numero di telefono, Gemma?
- **zero, sette, nove, due, sette, zero, cinque, uno, nove.**
- Paolo?
- **zero, cinque, nove, due, uno, sette, otto, quattro, tre.**

Gemma 079 270519; Paolo 059 217843

Page 20 Put it all together

1 *a* No, sono americana; *b* No, non sono italiano; *c* Sono di Milano; *d* No, io sono romano; *e* Sono infermiera.

2 Cognome: Manuzzi   Nome: Marco
Nazionalità: Italiano
Professione: Medico

3
- Mi **chiamo** Ulrike Schmitt. Sono **tedesca**, di Berlino e sono **dentista**.
- Mi chiamo Angela Roberts. Sono gallese, di Bangor e sono segretaria.
- Mi chiamo Marco Blondini. Sono italiano, di Roma, e sono ragioniere.

Page 21 Now you're talking!

1
- Scusi, dov'è il Municipio?
- **Non sono di qui.**
- Lei non è italiana?
- **No, sono inglese.**
- Di dov'è?
- **Sono di Chester. Di dov'è lei?**
- Sono veneziano.
- **Scusi?**
- Sono di Venezia – sono veneziano.

2
- Signor Fairlie, lei è inglese?
- **No, non sono inglese, sono scozzese.**
- Di dov'è?
- **Sono di Edimburgo.**
- Che lavoro fa?
- **Sono architetto.**

3
- Buongiorno! Come sta?
- **Bene, grazie.**
- Sono Pietro. Lei, come si chiama?
- **Mi chiamo + *your name*.**
- Lei è americano?
- **Sono + *your nationality*.**
- Di dov'è?
- **Sono di + *your home town*.**
- Che lavoro fa?
- **Sono + *your job*.**

Page 22 Quiz

1 Sono italiana; *2* Sono di Chester; *3* quattro, otto; *4* Di dov'è?; *5* Di dove sei? *6* Non sono di qui; *7* impiegato; *8* Florence; *9* Non.

Unit 3 Questo è Paolo

Pages 24 & 25 Introducing friends and family

2 • Buongiorno, signora Cesare.
• **Questo** è Paolo Lega.
• Piacere.
• E **questa** è Camilla Faldi.
• Piacere.

4 • Mario – questo è mio marito **Piero**.
• Piacere.
• Questa è **Marta**, mia moglie.
• Piacere, Marta.

5 • Sei sposata, Alessandra?
• Sono divorziata.
• Tu sei sposato, Ettore?
• Sì, sono sposato. E tu Mario, sei sposato tu?
• Io? No, non sono sposato. Sono single.
Mario è single; Alessandra è divorziata; Ettore è sposato.

7 • Hai bambini, Camilla?
• Sì, ho **un figlio** e **una figlia**.
• E tu, Marta, hai bambini?
• Ho **un figlio**. Roberto! . . . Questo è **mio figlio**.

8 • Renata, hai figli tu?
• Io? No, non sono sposata.
She's not married and she has no children.

9 • Questo è Enrico Piacenza.
• Questa è Francesca.
• Questo è mio marito . . . /Questa è mia moglie . . .

Pages 26 & 27 Saying how old you are and talking about your family

2 Quattordici (14).

3 quindici, cinquantacinque, dodici, quarantasei, ottantasette, settantatré.

5 • Ciao. Sono Laura. Questa è Marianna. Tu, come ti chiami?
• Massimo.
• Quanti anni hai?
• **Diciassette** – e tu?
• **Diciassette** anch'io.
• Quanti anni hai, Marianna?
• **Sedici.**
Massimo is 17; Laura is 17; Marianna is 16.

6 • Lei ha figli?
• Ho una **figlia**, Caterina, e ho anche un **figlio**.
• Come si **chiama**?
• Stefano.
• E quanti anni **ha**?
• Ha **undici** (11) anni.

7 • Mi chiamo Anna. Sono sposata e questo è Vittorio, mio marito. Questa è mia figlia Sofia. *(c)*
• Sono Alessandra Rossi. Io sono divorziata. Questa è mia figlia Caterina e questo è Stefano, mio figlio. *(a)*
• Mi chiamo Lorenzo. Non sono sposato. Questo è mio padre e questa è mia sorella Gianna. *(b)*

Page 28 Put it all together

1 *a* Mio padre si chiama Roberto; *b* Mia sorella si chiama Caterina; *c* Isabella è mia figlia; *d* Isabella ha 13 anni; *e* vero; *f* vero; *g* falso

2 gemelli – *twins*

Page 29 Now you're talking!

1 • Buongiorno, signora. Come si chiama?
• **Mi chiamo Anna Fraser.**
• Lei è sposata?
• **Sì, questo è mio marito Jonathan.**
• Ha figli?
• **Ho una figlia e un figlio.**
• Come si chiama sua figlia?
• **Si chiama Sarah.**

- Quanti anni ha?
- **Quattordici.**
- E suo figlio – come si chiama?
- **Si chiama Daniel.**
- Quanti anni ha?
- **Ha dodici anni.**

2
- Tu sei sposato?
- **Sì, sono sposato/a. / No, non sono sposato/a. E tu, sei sposato?**
- Sì, mia moglie si chiama Caterina.
- **Hai figli?**
- Sì – una figlia.
- **Come si chiama?**
- Laura.
- **Quanti anni ha?**
- Ha otto anni.
- **Questo/a è + *friend/partner's name.***
- Piacere.

Page 30 **Quiz**

1 questa è; 2 Anna, questo è mio fratello; 3 mia figlia; 4 sorella; 5 my father; 6 quanti anni hai? 7 ho . . . anni; 8 15

Unit 4 **Un caffè, per favore**

Pages 32 & 33 **Ordering a drink in a bar**

2
- Mi dica.
- **Una birra**, per favore.
- Una birra, signore. Va bene.

3
- Buongiorno. Prego?
- Un caffè, per favore.
- Una coca.
- Un caffè e una coca.
- Un gelato, per favore.
- Un'aranciata per me.
- Un caffè, una coca, un gelato e un'aranciata . . . va bene . . .
madre – caffè; padre – coca; figlia – gelato; figlio – aranciata

4
- Prego?
- **Un caffè**, per favore.
- Caffè **anche per me**.
- Con zucchero, Daniela?
- No, no, grazie – **senza** zucchero.

5
- Buona sera.
- Signora, buona sera. Mi dica.
- Un'acqua minerale, per favore.
- Gassata o non gassata?
- **Non gassata**. E un **cappuccino** per mia figlia.
- Allora, un **cappuccino** e un'acqua minerale **non gassata**. Va bene.

6
- Mi dica, signora.
- Un cappuccino, per favore.
- Signore?
- Un bicchiere di acqua minerale.
- Gassata o non gassata?
- Gassata.
- Zucchero, Anna?
- Sì, grazie.
a falso; *b* vero; *c* vero; *d* falso

7 un caffè, per favore; un gelato, per favore

Pages 34 & 35 **Offering someone a drink and accepting or refusing**

2
- Buongiorno, Mario.
- Ah, buongiorno, signor Guarino. Come sta?
- Bene, bene.
- Prende un caffè?
- **Sì, grazie.**
- Due caffè, per favore.
- Subito, signore.
- Luisa – buongiorno . . . un caffè?
- Sì, grazie – **un caffè macchiato.**

3
- Che cosa prendi, Claudia?
- Una birra.
- E tu, Fabio?
- Una birra anche per me.
- Allora, **tre birre**, per favore.

- Grazie.
- Prego.

They all order beer.

4
- Anita, che cosa prende?
- Un bicchiere di vino.
- Rosso o bianco?
- **Rosso**.
- Per lei, signora?
- Un bicchiere di **rosso** anche per me.
- Un bicchiere di vino **bianco** e due bicchieri di vino rosso.

Antonio – vino bianco; Anita and signora Perrone – vino rosso

5
- Signor Howard, che cosa prende?
- Come si dice in italiano 'whisky'?
- Whisky!
- Allora, **un whisky**.
- **Con ghiaccio?**
- **Sì**, grazie.
- Signor Guarino, prende **un whisky** anche lei?
- Volentieri.
- **Con ghiaccio?**
- **No – senza.**
- Allora, due whisky – uno con ghiaccio e uno senza – e **un Martini rosso**.
- Cin cin! Cin cin!

Signor Howard – con ghiaccio; Signor Guarino – senza ghiaccio; Mario – Martini rosso

Page 36 **Put it all together**

1 un caffè; un cappuccino; un tè; un'acqua minerale; un vino; una spremuta; una birra; una grappa; un gelato; un frullato; un'aranciata; un amaro

2
- Buongiorno, Antonia – prende un caffè?
- Volentieri – senza zucchero, per favore.
- E tu, Fabrizio, prendi un bicchiere di vino?
- No grazie – un caffè anche per me.
- Allora due caffè e un bicchiere di vino bianco per me.

3 Due birre e un cappuccino.
Due cappuccini e un caffè.
Due caffè e un bicchiere di vino.
Due aranciate e un gelato.

Page 37 **Now you're talking!**

1
- **Che cosa prendi, Emilio?**
- Un bicchiere di vino bianco.
- **Che cosa prendi, Francesca?**
- Un'aranciata, per favore.
- **Buongiorno, signora. Un bicchiere di vino bianco, un'aranciata e una birra, per favore.**

2
- Prende un caffè?
- **Volentieri. Un cappuchino, per favore.**
- Con zucchero?
- **Senza zucchero.**

3
- **Come si dice in italiano 'milk shake' ?**

4
- Buongiorno. Prego?
- **Due bicchieri di vino e due birre.**
- Vino bianco o rosso?
- **Rosso.**
- **Grazie – cin cin!**

Page 38 **Quiz**

1 zucchero; *2* caffè corretto; *3* con ghiaccio; *4* vini, birre, bicchieri; *5* a receipt; *6* masculine; *7* cin cin; *8* sparkling; *9* Sì, grazie, Volentieri; *10* Prego.

Punto di controllo 1 Pages 39 – 42

1
- Buongiorno, signora. Lei è qui in vacanza o per lavoro?
- **In vacanza.**
- Come si chiama?
- Laura Santoro.

- È italiana?
- No, non sono italiana, **sono americana**. Però, mio **padre è italiano** e io sono **in Italia con mia nonna**.
- Di dov'è?
- Sono **di San Diego**.
- È sposata?
- Sono **divorziata**.
- Ha bambini?
- Sì, ho **un figlio**.
- E che lavoro fa?
- Sono **disoccupata**.
- Grazie, signora. Arrivederci e buongiorno.

2
- Ciao. Come ti chiami?
- Caterina.
- Piacere. Io sono Jonathan.
- Tu non sei italiano, vero?
- **Sono irlandese**. Tu sei **italiana**?
- Sì. Sei in vacanza?
- No. Sono studente qui – a Perugia.
- Quanti anni hai?
- **Diciotto**. Quanti anni hai tu?
- **Diciannove**. Hai fratelli?
- Ho **due sorelle e un fratello**. E tu?
- Ho **una sorella**.

Caterina – Italian, 19, one sister. Jonathan – Irish, 18, two sisters and a brother.

3
- Che cosa prendi?
- Acqua minerale – gassata.
- Per favore – **un bicchiere di acqua minerale gassata** e **una birra**.
- Cin cin.
- Allora, arrivederci . . . Ecco il mio numero di telefono a Perugia: **zero, sette, cinque, sette, quattro, tre, zero, zero**.
- Il mio numero è **zero, sei, uno, otto, due, quattro, cinque, sei**.
- Arrivederci.

Caterina – sparkling mineral water, 0618 2456; Jonathan – beer, 075 74300.

5 Danimarca *(Denmark)* 19
Grecia *(Greece)* 75
Irlanda *(Ireland)* 99

Israele *(Israel)* **47**
Lussemburgo *(Luxemburg)* **72**
Norvegia *(Norway)* **12**
Olanda *(Holland)* **70**
Portogallo *(Portugal)* **83**

6 *a* Sì, grazie; *b* Prego; *c* Scusi? *d* Piacere; *e* Bene, grazie; *f* Cin cin.

7 *a* Come si chiama? / Come ti chiami?
b Quanti anni ha/hai?
c Che lavoro fa/fai?

8 birra, questo, lavoro, nonna, inglese, quanti, vino, prende, con, come
BUONGIORNO

9 Dear Rachel, my name's Alessandra Giardi and I'm Sicilian, from Siracusa. I'm 14. There are five of us in the family – my father Massimo who is unemployed, my mother Giuseppina who is a nurse at the hospital and my brother Stefano who is a student. Stefano is 19. There's also my grandmother . . .

Unit 5 **Scusi, dov'è la stazione?**

Pages 44 & 45 Asking where something is and asking for help to understand

2
- Allora Mario, **la stazione è qui**.
- Dov'è **il duomo**?
- **E lì**.
- E **la questura**, dov'è?
- **È dietro il municipio**.
- Dov'è **l'azienda di turismo**?
- **In centro città** – qui.
- E dov'è **l'ufficio postale**?
- . . . **è in via della Vittoria**.
- È lontano?
- Sì . . . No . . . dieci minuti a piedi.

La stazione è qui.
Il duomo è lì.
L'azienda di turismo è in centro città.

La questura è dietro il municipio.
L'ufficio postale è in via della Vittoria.

4 ● Scusi, signore, dov'è il Municipio?
● È in Piazza Garibaldi, in centro.
● Può ripetere, per favore?
● È in Piazza Garibaldi . . . non è qui, è in centro . . .
● Grazie. Può parlare lentamente?
● **È in centro, lontano da qui . . . venti minuti a piedi.**
It's in the centre, a long way away, twenty minutes' walk.

5 ● Scusi, **dove sono** i negozi?
● Sono lì, **in centro**.
● È lontano il centro?
● No, no – a **500 metri, cinque minuti a piedi**.
● Può ripetere per favore?
● Cinque minuti a piedi – 500 metri.
In the centre, 500 m. away; 5 minutes.

6 Dov'è l'azienda di turismo?
Dov'è l'ufficio postale?
Dov'è la stazione?
Dove sono i negozi?

Pages 46 & 47 Talking about where you live and work

2 ● Signora, abita qui a Bologna?
● Abito **in periferia**.
● Abita qui a Bologna, signore?
● Sì – abito qui **in centro città**.
● Scusi signora, dove abita?
● Lontano da qui – **in campagna**.
sig.ra 1 – in periferia; sig. – in centro; sig.ra 2 – in campagna.

3/4
● Signora Bonino, dove abita?
● Io abito qui a Bologna, in una casa, viale Roma **34**.
● E lei, signor Quarta, abita qui?
● Sì, in un appartamento. Piazza Garibaldi, numero **6**.
● Signora Galli, anche lei abita in un appartamento?

● Sì, ho un appartamento in un palazzo in via Verdi **27**. E mia figlia abita in una villetta in via Aurelia **53**.
sig. Bonino – viale Roma 34; sig. Quarta – piazza Garibaldi 6; sig.ra Galli – via Verdi 27; la figlia di Caterina –via Aurelia 53.

7 ● **Signora Galli**, dove lavora?
● Lavoro nella zona industriale – **per la Zanussi**.
● E tu, **Luciano**, dove lavori?
● Lavoro **in un ufficio** in centro.
● E tu, Franca?
● Io non lavoro.
Signora Galli works for Zanussi.
Luciano works in an office.

8 ● Scusi, dove lavora?
● Per la Fiat. *(1)*
● Dove lavora lei?
● In una pizzeria in centro. *(2)*
● E lei, dove lavora?
● Lavoro in un ufficio in via Puccini. *(3)*
● Scusi, signora, dove lavora?
● A Roma – abito e lavoro a Roma. *(4)*
● Dove lavori?
● Non lavoro – sono studente. *(5)*
He's a student.

Page 48 Put it all together

1 *a* il, i, la; *b* la, l', l'; *c* il, l', la; *d* la, il, i

2 *a* È in centro; *b* Lavoro in Via Marconi; *c* Sì, abito qui; *d* Sono in centro; *e* No, lavoro in centro; *f* Cinque minuti a piedi.

3 **a** Firenze; **in** un negozio **in** piazza Garibaldi; **in** una pizzeria **a** Milano; **in** un ufficio **in** via Manzini; **a** Roma **a** with towns; **in** with buildings, streets and squares, countries, islands

4 appartamento, duecento, municipio, gli, periferia

1 ● **Buongiorno, signora, dov'è il duomo?**
  ● Il duomo? È in centro – in Piazza Duomo.
  ● **È lontano?**
  ● No, no, dieci minuti a piedi.
  ● **E dov'è il municipio?**
  ● È dietro il Duomo.
  ● **Scusi? Può ripetere, per favore?**

2 ● **Dove sono i negozi?**
  ● Sono in via Michelangelo, a due passi.
  ● **Può parlare più lentamente?**
  ● In via Michelangelo, a due passi . . . non è lontano.
  ● **Grazie signore.**

3 ● Lei è tedesco?
  ● **No, sono + your nationality.**
  ● Dove abita?
  ● **Abito a + your town.**
  ● Abita in centro città?
  ● **No, abito + where you live.**
  ● E dove lavora?
  ● e.g. **Lavoro a Londra, per la BBC.**

4 ● **Abita qui?**
  ● No, lavoro qui ma abito in via Belloni.
  ● **Dov'è via Belloni?**
  ● Non è lontano – è in periferia, a quindici minuti da qui.

Page 50 **Quiz**

1 qui; *2* dov'è? – where is?, dove sono? – where are? *3* behind the station; *4* abita in periferia; *5* la birra, il figlio, l'Italia; *6* the old part of town; *7* quattrocento; *8* non

Unit 6 **C'è una banca qui vicino?**

Pages 52 & 53 **Understanding what there is in town and when it's open**

2 banca *bank*; albergo *hotel*; mercato *market*; museo *museum*; stazione *station*; piscina *swimming pool*; supermercato *supermarket*; farmacia *chemist's*; ristorante *restaurant*; teatro *theatre*.

3 ● Ecco l'azienda di promozione turistica qui. In città c'è un **teatro** e un **museo**. C'è il **mercato** in centro e ci sono anche tre **supermercati**. Ci sono **trattorie** e molti **ristoranti**.
  ● Dov'è la **piscina**?
  ● Non c'è una piscina qui, ma ce n'è una a Forlini, a 15 chilometri da qui.
  ● Dov'è la **stazione**?
  ● La stazione è in centro – non è lontano da qui. Ecco una piantina, signore.

4 ● *a* falso; *b* vero; *c* vero; *d* vero

6 ● La piscina è aperta **ogni giorno**. **Lunedì** e **venerdì** c'è un mercato in Piazza Marconi in centro. Il museo è chiuso **oggi**; è aperto **martedì**, **giovedì** e **sabato**. L'azienda di turismo è chiusa **domenica**.

Pages 54 & 55 **Making simple enquiries and understanding directions**

2 ● Scusi, c'è un telefono qui?
  ● Ecco **qui a sinistra**.
  ● Grazie. C'è una toilette?
  ● **Lì in fondo a destra**, signora.

3 ● Scusi, signore, c'è una banca qui vicino?
  ● Mi dispiace, **non lo so** – non sono di qui.

4 ● Scusi, signore, c'è una banca qui vicino?
  ● Sì, in via Mazzini – **a destra** e poi a sinistra.
  ● A destra poi a sinistra. Grazie.
  Right and then left.

5 ● Scusi, signore, c'è una farmacia qui vicino?
  ● Giorgio, c'è una farmacia qui vicino?
  ● Ce n'è una in via Vittoria Emanuele – **a sinistra, la prima a destra poi sempre dritto.**

- Può ripetere, per favore?
- A sinistra, la prima a destra poi sempre dritto.
Left, first right, straight on.

6 • Scusi, signora, dov'è l'azienda di turismo?
- **In Corso Italia – in centro. È** lontano da qui.
- È aperta oggi?
- **Non lo so**, mi dispiace.
- C'è un autobus?
- Sì – c'è il **sedici**.
- Grazie.
We don't know if it's open. Bus no. 16.

7 • Scusi, signore, dov'è l'azienda di turismo?
- Sempre dritto fino al semaforo – **cinquecento metri** – poi **a destra**.
500 m.; right at lights.

8 • Buongiorno. C'è un mercato qui?
- Sì c'è un mercato martedì e venerdì in Piazza Italia.
- C'è un museo?
- Ci sono due musei; tutti e due sono chiusi domenica.
- C'è una piscina?
- Sì, in via Garibaldi.
- È aperta oggi?
- È aperta ogni giorno, signora.
- Ci sono magazzini?
- Sì, in centro. Sono aperti da lunedì a sabato, e chiusi domenica.
- Grazie. Arrivederci.
a falso; b vero; c vero; d vero; e vero; f falso

9 C'è una banca qui vicino?
C'è una farmacia qui vicino?
C'è un ristorante qui vicino?
C'è un supermercato qui vicino?

Page 56 **Put it all together**

I *a* Monday; *b* Yes, mornings only; *c* every day; *d* Tuesday

Page 57 **Now you're talking!**

I • **Scusi, signore, c'è una farmacia qui vicino?**
- Una farmacia . . . sì, a sinistra poi sempre dritto.
- **A sinistra, poi sempre dritto. Grazie.**

2 • **Scusi, c'è un supermercato qui vicino?**
- C'è l'ipermercato a Molinella . . . ma è lontano.
- **C'è un autobus?**
- Sì, deve prendere il numero quarantadue.
- **Il quarantadue. Grazie signora. Arrivederci.**

3 • **C'è un bar qui vicino?**
- Lì a sinistra – ecco.
- **Grazie; c'è un albergo qui vicino?**
- Mi dispiace, non lo so.
- **Dov'è l'azienda di turismo?**
- A destra, sempre dritto duecento metri, poi la prima a sinistra.
- **A destra, sempre dritto duecento metri, poi la prima a sinistra. È aperta?**
- Sì, sì.

4 • **Ci sono ristoranti qui vicino?**
- In via Doria, c'è la Trattoria Corallo.
- **È lontano?**
- No, no . . . cinque minuti a piedi.

Page 58 **Quiz**

I Tourist information office; 2 right; 3 ristorante, trattoria, pizzeria; 4 C'è un telefono? 5 closed; 6 c'è; 7 sabato (Sat) and domenica (Sun); 8 a map; 9 non lo so.

Unit 7 **Quanto costa?**

Pages 60 & 61 **Understanding prices and asking for items in a shop**

2 a € 13 b € 0,75 c € 24,99 d € 82
e € 12,25 f € 350

4 una guida di Firenze *guidebook of
Florence*; tre cartoline *postcards*;
un giornale inglese *English newspaper*;
tre francobolli *stamps*; una carta
telefonica *telephone card*; cerotti
plasters.

5 ● Buongiorno. Dica.
● Signora, quanto **costa** questa guida?
● **Dieci** euro (€ 10).
● E quanto **costano** i giornali inglesi?
● **Un euro e quindici** (€ 1,15).

6 ● Buongiorno, mi dica.
● **Quanto costano i cerotti?**
● Cerotti . . . questi costano € 2,49.

7 ● Scusi, quanto costano le cartoline?
● Trenta centesimi.
● Quanto costa un francobollo per la
Gran Bretagna?
● Quarantuno.
● E un francobollo per gli Stati Uniti?
● Cinquanta due centesimi.
● Avete carte telefoniche?
● Mi dispiace, no.
*cartolina € 0,30; francobollo per la Gran
Bretagna € 0,41; francobollo per gli Stati
Uniti € 0,52.*

8 ● Buongiorno. Dica.
● Avete biglietti per l'autobus?
● Sì, certo.
● Quanto costano?
● Un euro e dieci il biglietto.
● Mi dà quattro, no cinque biglietti.
● Cinque e cinquanta, signore.
● Grazie. Quattro euro e cinquanta di
resto. Arrivederci, signore.
*One ticket – € 1,10; he buys five tickets;
change € 4,50.*

9 Avete francobolli? Avete una guida?
Avete biglietti per l'autobus? Quanto
costa una cartolina? Quanto costano i

biglietti per l'autobus? Quanto costa un
giornale inglese?

Pages 62 & 63 **Shopping for food in the
market**

1 Allora . . . sei panini, mezzo chilo di
formaggio, un etto di prosciutto, mezzo
litro di olio di oliva, un litro di acqua
minerale, una bottiglia di vino rosso e
una bottiglia di vino bianco e un
chilo di zucchero.

3 ● Buongiorno, signora. Mi dica.
● Mi dà un litro di acqua minerale.
● Gassata o non gassata?
● Gassata . . . e due bottiglie di vino,
bianco e rosso.
● Acqua minerale, gassata, due bottiglie
di vino. Altro?
● Mezzo chilo di formaggio . . . un etto
di prosciutto . . . e quanto costa l'olio
di oliva extra vergine?
● € 7,50 il litro, € 4,00 mezzo litro.
● Ne prendo mezzo litro.
● Basta così?
● No – mi dà sei panini . . . e basta.
● 28 euro e 20, signora.
Still to buy: a kilo of sugar.

4 ● Buongiorno. Vorrei un **chilo di
mele** e un chilo di banane.
● . . . Altro?
● Mi dà **mezzo chilo di pomodori** e
250 grammi di funghi.
● Mezzo chilo di pomodori e 250
grammi di funghi. Basta così?
● Quanto costano le fragole?
● 6 euro il mezzo chilo. Ne vuole?
● No, basta così, grazie.
*1 kg. apples; 250g. mushrooms; half kg.
tomatoes*

5 ● Vorrei mezzo chilo di questi
pomodori.
● Prendo **queste** banane.
● Mi dà **due chili** di patate.
● Una di queste **pesche**, per favore.

6 panini, formaggio, prosciutto, due bottiglie di vino, acqua minerale, frutta e verdura, olio di oliva, **mezzo chilo di caffè** . . . e basta.
Half a kilo of coffee

7 Mi dà . . . mezzo chilo di queste mele; tre pesche; un litro di acqua minerale; una bottiglia di vino rosso.

Page 64 **Put it all together**

1 *a* I'd like; *b* Could you give me? *c* That's all; *d* How much is it? *e* Do you have? *f* Anything else? *g* How much are they?

2 **pizza:** pomodori, funghi, formaggio, sale, pepe, olio di oliva, farina
macedonia: fragole, arance, zucchero, pesche, banane, mele, limone
patate (potatoes) left over

3 panini; formaggio, prosciutto; pomodori; banane; mele; due bottigli di vino; una bottiglia di acqua minerale

4 € 18,00; € 14,25; € 10,75
change € 7,00

Page 65 **Now you're talking!**

1 ● Buongiorno. Dica.
● **Un chilo di mele e mezzo chilo di banane.**
● Altro?
● **Mezzo chilo di pomodori.**
● Basta?
● **Sì, basta così, grazie.**

2 ● **Mi dà quattro panini.**
● E poi?
● **Vorrei una bottiglia di vino rosso e un litro di acqua minerale gassata.**
● Altro?
● **Un etto di prosciutto.**
● Quale?
● **Questo qui.**

● Basta così?
● **Basta così, grazie.**

3 ● Buongiorno. Dica.
● **Quanto costa un francobollo per la Gran Bretagna?**
● Quarantuno centesimi.
● **Prendo due cartoline e due francobolli.**
● Altro?
● **Quanto costano i biglietti per l'autobus?**
● Cinquantuno.
● **Vorrei sei biglietti e una carta telefonica.**

Page 66 **Quiz**

1 costano, costano, costa; *2* 555; *3* 10; *4* tobacconist's; *5* un giornale italiano; *6* un francobollo per l'Australia; *7* questi; *8* mezzo

Punto di controllo 2 Pages 67 – 70

1

a ● Scusi signora, c'è una banca qui vicino?
● Sempre dritto fino al semaforo poi giri a sinistra . . .
● Può parlare lentamente? Non sono italiano.
● Allora – sempre dritto, poi al semaforo giri a sinistra e in viale Torricelli c'è la Banca Popolare, a destra.

b ● Scusi, dov'è la stazione?
● Mi dispiace, non lo so – non sono di qui.
● Scusi, dov'è la stazione?
● Giri a destra al semaforo, poi prenda la prima a sinistra, cioè via Quattro Novembre, continui sempre dritto e la stazione è in fondo.
● È lontano?
● No, no – cinquecento metri.

c • C'è una farmacia qui?
• Ce n'è una in via Cavour: sempre dritto, la prima a sinistra, poi la prima a destra. C'è una farmacia a destra fra la banca e l'ufficio postale.
a bank E; *b* station A; *c* chemist C

2 *a* C'è un **bar** e un'**edicola** in piazza Italia.
b **L'azienda di turismo** è a sinistra del mercato.
c La **farmacia** è fra la banca e l'ufficio postale.

3 Roma **613 km.**; Firenze **325 km.**; Napoli **831 km.**; Bari **915 km.**

4 Il prosciutto di Parma costa € **3,50**.
L'olio di oliva costa € **8,95**.
Le olive costano € **2,20**.
I pomodori costano € **0,99**.
Il pane costa € **1,00**.
Il formaggio costa € **3,79**.

5 *a* edicola; *b* mercato; *c* farmacia; *d* tabaccheria; *e* azienda di turismo; *f* caffè

6 *a* domenica; *b* cerotti; *c* villa; *d* patata

7 *a* Può parlare lentamente? *b* Non sono di qui; *c* Non lo so; *d* Come si dice in italiano? *e* Può ripetere per favore? *f* Mi dispiace.

8 formaggio / pizza; lire / banca; piscina / acqua; ristorante / trattoria; francobollo / cartolina; appartamento / casa; edicola / giornale; professione / lavoro

9 *a* **questi** funghi; *b* **questa** cartolina? *c* **questo** vino; *d* **queste** pesche; *e* **questo** ristorante; *f* **queste** fragole.

10 *a* falso; *b* falso; *c* vero; *d* falso; *e* vero; *f* vero; *g* falso

Unit 8 **Vorrei una camera**

Page 72 **Checking in at reception**

2 • Buona sera, signora. Mi chiamo Enzo Pittara. Ho prenotato una camera.
• Buona sera, signore. Allora . . . **una camera singola, con bagno**. Sì. **Camera numero 256 – secondo piano.** Ecco la chiave.
• Grazie.

• Buona sera. Sono Stella Rossini.
• Ah . . . **camera doppia – matrimoniale – con bagno**?
• Sì, esatto.
• **Camera numero 124 al primo piano**, signora.
• C'è l'ascensore?
• Ecco – in fondo a destra. Il suo passaporto per favore.

• Buona sera, signora. Ho prenotato una camera – una camera doppia.
• Il suo nome?
• Barucci.
• Ah signor Barucci – **una camera a due letti al pianterreno**. Ecco la chiave – **camera numero 65**.
sig. Pittara – single, bath, room 256, 2nd floor; sig.ra Rossini – double bed, bath, room 124, 1st floor; sig. Barucci – twin beds, room 65, ground floor.

3 **In fondo a destra** (at the end on the right)

Page 73 **Finding a hotel room**

2/4
• Buona sera.
• Buona sera. Avete una camera per stasera?
• Singola o doppia?
• Singola, con bagno.
• **Solo per stasera?**
• Sì.
• Va bene – camera singola con bagno per una notte. Il suo nome?

- Bagli.
- Come si scrive?
- **BAGLI.**

- Buona sera. Vorrei una camera doppia per tre notti.
- Tre notti . . . allora, fino a venerdì. Un attimo, signore . . . Sì, va bene. Il suo nome?
- Theaker.
- Come si scrive?
- **THEAKER.**
for three nights

3 Alberto **CENCI**.

6 Vorrei una camera . . .
   . . . singola con doccia per stasera
   . . . doppia con bagno per tre notti
   . . . a due letti per una settimana
   . . . singola senza bagno fino a domenica

Page 74 **Booking ahead by phone**

2

a ● Pronto. Hotel San Marco. Buongiorno.
   ● Buongiorno. Vorrei prenotare una camera.
   ● Sì, per quando?
   ● Per sabato il **12 luglio**.
   ● Un attimo . . . Mi dispiace, siamo al completo.
   ● Grazie, buongiorno.

b ● Pronto. Hotel San Marco.
   ● Buongiorno. Vorrei prenotare una camera singola con bagno.
   ● Per quando?
   ● Il 14 settembre.
   ● Per una notte?
   ● No, per due notti – **il 14 e il 15 settembre**.
   ● D'accordo. Un attimo.

c ● Pronto. Buongiorno. Vorrei prenotare una camera.
   ● Sì – per quando?
   ● Per una settimana in aprile – **dal 13 al 20 aprile**.

- Una camera singola o doppia?
- Doppia . . . con bagno.
- A due letti o matrimoniale?
- Matrimoniale . . .
a 12 July; b 14–15 September;
c 13–20 April

Page 75 **Making requests**

2 ● Buongiorno, signora. Posso **lasciare la valigia qui**?
   ● Certo, **signor Belloni**. S'accomodi.

   ● Signora, sono **Luigi Ciani**. Vorrei telefonare a New York. **Posso telefonare da qui**?
   ● Sì, signore. Il telefono è lì sulla destra.
   ● E **posso pagare con la carta di credito**?
   ● Sì, sì.

   ● Scusi, **posso parlare con il direttore**?
   ● Il suo nome?
   ● **Lorna Tonino.**
   ● Un attimo, signora Tonino.

   ● Buongiorno, signora. Vorrei una camera singola per stasera.
   ● Con bagno? Abbiamo solo una singola senza bagno.
   ● **Posso vedere la camera**?
   ● Certo – un attimo . . . Il suo nome, per favore?
   ● **Chini.** CHINI.
   sig. Belloni – leave a suitcase
   L. Tonino – speak to the manager
   L. Ciani – telephone / pay by credit card
   sig. Chini – see the room

3 ● Scusi, possiamo parcheggiare qui?
   ● No, mi dispiace – qui no – ma **c'è un parcheggio dietro l'albergo**. La targa della sua macchina?
   ● **FI 35782.**
   behind the hotel

Page 76 **Put it all together**

1 *a* I'd like to book; *b* I've booked; *c* Have you got? *d* Can I? *e* Can we? *f* Hello

2 *a* Ho prenotato una camera singola;
  b Vorrei una camera singola con doccia;
  c Avete una camera a due letti?
  d Ha una camera matrimoniale con bagno per una notte?
  e Vorrei prenotare una camera matrimoniale per il 21 marzo.
  f Posso telefonare?

3 *a* Sì; *b* Sì; *c* Sì; *d* No; *e* No

Page 77 Now you're talking!

I ● Buongiorno, signora. Mi dica.
  ● **Avete una camera?**
  ● Singola o doppia?
  ● **Singola, con bagno.**
  ● Per quante notti?
  ● **Per stasera.**
  ● Va bene, signora – camera numero 245 al secondo piano.
  ● **Posso vedere la camera?**
  ● Certo, signora . . .

2 ● **Buongiorno, signora, ho prenotato una camera.**
  ● Il suo nome, signore?
  ● **Mi chiamo John Graham.**
  ● Allora, una camera doppia con bagno.
  ● **No, una camera singola con bagno.**
  ● . . . per tre notti?
  ● **No, per due notti – fino al 22 agosto.**
  ● Che strano. Come si scrive il suo nome?
  ● **GRAHAM.**
  ● Ah signore – sì, scusi – camera singola per due notti.
  ● **Posso pagare con la carta di credito?**
  ● Sì, certo.

Page 78 Quiz

1 camera, chiave; 2 agosto; *3* May 1st; *4* first floor; *5* breakfast; *6* car registration number; *7* posso – I, possiamo – we; *8* no

Unit 9 A che ora parte?

Page 80 Asking about public transport

2 ● Scusi, c'è **un autobus per la stazione**?
  ● Ce n'è uno ogni mezz'ora.
  ● Quando parte?
  ● Ce n'è uno **alle 10.00.**

  ● C'è **un autobus per piazza Garibaldi**?
  ● **Ogni mezz'ora**, signore. Numero 25.
  ● Ce n'è uno alle dieci?
  ● **Alle 10.00** – sì.

  ● C'è **un pullman per l'aeroporto**?
  ● Ce n'è uno **ogni ora**.
  ● Quando parte?
  ● Ce n'è uno **alle 11.00**, signora.
  bus to Piazza Garibaldi – every half hour, 10:00; coach to airport – every hour, 11:00.

3 C'è un pullman per l'aeroporto?
  C'è un autobus per la stazione?
  Ce n'è uno alle dieci?

Page 81 Finding out train times

2 ● A che ora parte il prossimo treno per Roma?
  ● **Alle 8 e 18.**
  ● Grazie.

  ● Scusi, c'è un treno per Bologna?
  ● Ce n'è **uno ogni due ore**.
  ● A che ora parte il prossimo?
  ● **Alle 9 e 34**.
  ● Grazie.

  ● A che ora parte il prossimo treno per Bergamo?
  ● Alle **10 e 12.**
  ● E a che ora arriva a Bergamo?
  ● Alle **10 e 54**.
  ● Scusi, a che ora arriva il treno da Venezia?

- Arriva alle **8 e 25**.
- E il treno da Padova – a che ora arriva?
- Alle **9 e 12**.
- Grazie.

Roma – 8.18; Bologna – 9.34; Bergamo – 10.12; Venezia – 8.25; Padova – 9.12.

3 *a* falso; *b* falso.

4 A che ora parte il prossimo treno per Firenze?
A che ora arriva a Firenze?
A che ora arriva il treno da Venezia?

Pages 82 & 83 Buying tickets and checking travel details

2
- **Bologna**, **andata e ritorno**. Grazie.

- Mi dà un **andata per Milano**.
- Prima o seconda classe?
- **Seconda.**
- 35 euro
- Grazie.

- Due biglietti per **Verona, andata e ritorno** . . . e in **prima classe**. Grazie.
- **Binario 5.**

- Vorrei un biglietto per **Firenze, con supplemento Intercity**.
- Solo andata o andata e ritorno?
- Solo **andata**.

- **Roma, andata e ritorno, con supplemento rapido.** Grazie. Da che binario parte?
- **Binario 12.**

Bologna – return; Milano – single, second; Verona – return, first; Firenze – single, supplement; Roma – return, supplement

3 *a* Verona, Bin. 5; *b* Roma, Bin. 12.

5
- A che ora parte il prossimo treno per Napoli?
- Alle nove e diciassette.
- È diretto?

- No, **deve cambiare** a Roma.

Deve cambiare? Sì

6
- C'è un treno per Arezzo?
- Ce n'è uno alle otto e venti.
- Può ripetere, per favore?
- **C'è un treno che parte alle otto e venti.**
- Devo cambiare?
- No, **è diretto** – è l'Intercity – **deve prenotare il posto**.
- Non capisco.
- Il treno è l'Intercity e lei deve prenotare il posto.
- Quanto costa?
- € 45,70 e c'è un supplemento di € 10,60 che fanno € **56,30**.
- Scusi . . . non capisco . . .

at 8.20; he doesn't have to change; ticket costs € 56,30; he has to make a seat reservation

7
- Dove posso comprare un biglietto per l'autobus?
- **Deve** andare in tabaccheria – ce n'è una lì, a destra.
- Grazie.
- Scusi, **devo** scendere qui per il Duomo?
- No, alla prossima fermata.
- Grazie.

Page 84 Put it all together

1 *a* 2; *b* 5; *c* 6; *d* 3; *e* 4; *f* 1

2 *a* alle sette; *b* alle diciannove; *c* alle undici; *d* alle ventitré; *e* alle otto e venticinque; *f* alle venti e venticinque

3 *a* Mi dà un biglietto di seconda classe.
b C'è un autobus ogni venti minuti.
c Deve scendere alla seconda fermata.
d Il prossimo treno parte alle nove e venti.
e Il biglietto costa ventidue euro.

4 *a* Devo cambiare? *b* Devo prenotare?
c Devo scendere qui?

Page 85 **Now you're talking!**

1 • **C'è un pullman per Perugia?**
  • Ce n'è uno ogni due ore.
  • **A che ora parte il prossimo?**
  • Alle dieci.
  • **Devo prenotare?**
  • No, non è necessario.
  • **Quanto costa il biglietto?**
  • Andata o andata e ritorno?
  • **Andata e ritorno.**
  • Quattordici euro.

2 • **A che ora parte il prossimo treno per Orvieto?**
  • Orvieto . . . alle nove e quaranta.
  • **A che ora arriva a Orvieto?**
  • Alle dieci e quarantasette.
  • **Devo cambiare?**
  • No, è diretto.
  • **Vorrei un biglietto di andata e ritorno.**
  • Prima o seconda classe?
  • **Seconda classe. Da che binario parte?**
  • Binario numero quattro.
  • **Grazie.**

3 • **Scusi, signora, a che ora parte il prossimo autobus per il centro?**
  • Alle otto e venticinque.
  • **C'è una tabaccheria qui vicino?**
  • Ce n'è una in via Puccini – a destra al semaforo. *(There's one in via Puccini – on the right at the lights.)*

Page 86 **Quiz**

1 ogni; *2* Non capisco; *3* fast trains on which you pay a supplement and need a seat reservation; *4* you have to do something; *5* 6 p.m.; *6* return; *7* non fumatori; *8* from Rome

Unit 10 **Buon appetito!**

Page 90 **Asking about items on the menu**

2 • Buongiorno, signori.
  • Buongiorno.
  • Tavolo per **tre**?
  • Siamo in tre, sì.
  • Aperitivi?
  • Una bottiglia di **vino bianco** della regione.
  • E una **birra**.

3/4
  • Allora, signori, per primo abbiamo **zuppa**, **minestrone**, **cannelloni al forno,** spaghetti al pomodoro o alla carbonara e **risotto**.
  • Cos'è la zuppa del giorno?
  • È una **zuppa di carote**.
  • Com'è il risotto?
  • Ai funghi.
  • E come sono gli spaghetti alla carbonara?
  • Sono spaghetti . . . fatti con uova, **prosciutto**, panna, **formaggio** e pepe.
  • Grazie.

5 Com'è il risotto?
  Come sono i ravioli?

Page 91 **Ordering a meal**

2 • Allora, cosa prendono per primo?
  • **Per me** il minestrone.
  • Io **prendo** il risotto ai funghi . . . e le tagliatelle al ragù **per** mia figlia.
  • Da bere?
  • Una bottiglia di acqua minerale e una caraffa di vino bianco.
  • Un litro?
  • No, mezzo litro.

3 • Pronta per ordinare, signora? Cosa prende per primo?
  • **No, niente primo**, grazie.
  • Allora, per secondo?
  • Che cosa c'è?
  • Allora . . . abbiamo pesce, filetto di maiale e l'agnello.
  • Com'è l'agnello?
  • Arrosto – con aglio e rosmarino.
  • Che cosa consiglia?

L'agnello è buono oggi – molto buono.
Allora prendo **l'agnello**.
E come contorno?
Zucchini.
Agnello con zucchini . . . Va bene.

4 . . . e da bere, signora?
Mezzo litro di acqua minerale – **non gassata** – e una caraffa di **rosso**.
Mezzo litro? Un quarto?
Un **quarto**.
Ecco, signora. Buon appetito.

5 Prendo il pesce e l'insalata.

Pages 92 & 93 Saying what you like and don't like, and paying compliments

2 **Signore, per favore.**
Dolci, signori? Abbiamo **fragole, gelati, formaggi, torta di mele** – una specialità della casa . . .
Io vorrei assaggiare un formaggio della regione. Mi piace il formaggio.
No . . . non mi piace il formaggio. Prendo la torta al cioccolato.
Niente dolce per me.
. . . formaggio e torta al cioccolato. Grazie.

3 Ecco la torta . . . per lei, signora?
No, è per me la torta.
. . . e il formaggio. Questo è dolcelatte, un formaggio della regione. Le piace, signora?
Sì, **mi piace**, mi piace molto.
Posso assaggiare?
Sì, certo . . . ti piace?
Mm – è buono, **è buonissimo**.
Angela?
Grazie no, **non mi piace** il formaggio.
sig.ra 1 – likes; sig. – likes;
sig.ra 2 – doesn't like

4 Mi piace il vino bianco.
Mi piace il formaggio.

6 Tutto bene, signori?
Sì grazie, è **delizioso – complimenti!**
Che buono!

Le piace il formaggio, signora?
Sì – è buonissimo.
Le piacciono i formaggi italiani allora?
Mi piacciono tutti i formaggi!
E, tutto bene, signora?
Sì, grazie, la torta al cioccolato **è deliziosa.**

7 Torta di mele per me.
Anche per me.
E anche per me. Allora, **torta di mele per tutti**.
È buona questa torta. Ti piace, Luisa?
Mi piace molto. Mi piacciono le mele. Mi piace anche il cioccolato.
They all choose apple tart.

8 Mi piacciono le fragole.
Mi piacciono le mele.

Page 94 Put it all together

1 *a* of the house; *b* grilled; *c* fried; *d* in season; *e* of the day; *f* baked; *g* with tomatoes

2 *primi* – risotto, ravioli, zuppa
secondi – coniglio, vitello, agnello
contorni – patate, insalata, zucchini
dolci – gelato, sorbetto, torta

3 *a* Mi piace il prosciutto.
b Mi piacciono le tagliatelle al ragù.
c Mi piace il risotto alla marinara.
d Mi piace il vitello ai funghi.
e Mi piace la torta di mele.
f Mi piacciono le fragole.
To say you don't like them, add **non** *before* **mi**.

4 *a* ottimo; *b* buonissimi; *c* squisita; *d* buone; *e* deliziosa

Page 95 Now you're talking!

1 Buongiorno, signori. Tavolo per due?
Sì, per due.
Ecco il menù.
Grazie.

- Pronti per ordinare?
- **Sì – un risotto alla marinara e i cannelloni.**
- E per secondo?
- **Cosa consiglia?**
- Il pesce è buono oggi – molto buono.
- **Il pesce e il pollo all'aglio.**
- E come contorno?
- **Patate e zucchini.**

- Ecco . . . pesce . . . e pollo. Buon appetito.
- **Vorrei una caraffa di vino rosso.**
- Un litro?
- **Mezzo litro.**

- Tutto bene? Le piace il pesce?
- **Sì, mi piace, è buonissimo.**
- Dessert, signori?
- **Cosa è la torta della casa?**
- È una torta di pere con panna. Le piacciono le pere?
- **Mi piacciono molto ma non mi piace la panna.**
- **Prendo un gelato e il formaggio.**
- Va bene.

Page 96 **Quiz**

1 Un tavolo per due; *2* garlic; *3* mi piacciono; *4* Niente dolce per me; *5* Signore, per favore! *6* agnello; *7* buonissimo; *8* maiale; *9* Buon appetito!

Controllo finale Pages 97 – 100

1 *c* Scusi, c'è un bar qui vicino?

2 • **Un'acqua minerale per favore – con ghiaccio.**
- Un euro e ottantadue. Ecco lo scontrino.
- **Grazie, signora.**
a € 8,18; *b* a till receipt

3 *a* Posso telefonare da qui?
b Dov'è la toilette?
c L'azienda di turismo è aperta oggi?
d Quanto costano le cartoline?

4 • Dov'è l'Hotel Arcangelo?
- L'Hotel Arcangelo? . . . Prenda la prima a sinistra, al primo semaforo giri a destra – via Michelangelo – e l'Arcangelo è in fondo a destra.
1st left, right at the lights, into via Michelangelo, hotel is at the end on the right.

5 *a* A che ora parte il primo treno per Roma martedì?
b A che ora arriva a Roma?
c Quanto costa un biglietto di andata?

6 *d* Ho prenotato una camera singola con doccia fino a martedì.

7 • Scusi, **come si scrive il suo nome**? Grazie . . . camera 134 al **primo piano. Mi dà il passaporto**, per favore.
a *How do you spell your name?*
b *Could you give me your passport?*
c *Room 134* *d* *first floor.*

8 • Il cambio oggi per la sterlina . . . vediamo . . . € 1,66.

9 • Viaggio molto . . . domani e martedì lavoro a Firenze; martedì sera vado a Milano fino a giovedì mattina. Poi altri due giorni in Germania e, finalmente, domenica, vado in Francia – a casa!
lunedì *Firenze;* **martedì** *Firenze e Milano (sera);* **mercoledì** *Milano;* **giovedì** *Milano / Germania;* **venerdì** *Germania;* **sabato** *Germania;* **domenica** *Francia*

10 *a* Mi chiamo Paul Durand. *b* No, sono francese. *c* Abito a Nizza in Francia. *d* È sposato? *e* Come si chiama sua moglie? *f* Ha figli? *g* Quanti anni ha? *h* Che lavoro fa? *i* Parla inglese? *j* Le piace lo sport?

11 240 euro; Duecentoquaranta euro.

12 *a* grilled meat and fish; *b* no; *c* local; *d* home cooking

Grammar

Grammar is simply the term used to describe the patterns of a language. Knowing these patterns will enable you to move away from total reliance on set phrases.

I **Nouns** (words for people, things, places, concepts) are all either masculine (m.) or feminine (f.) in Italian.

Singular nouns (one only)	**To form the Plural** (more than one)
a ending in -**o**: (nearly always m.)	-**o** changes to -**i**
b ending in -**a**: (usually f.)	-**a** changes to -**e**
c ending in -**e**: (some m., some f.)	-**e** changes to -**i**

2 **Adjectives** (words which describe) have to 'agree' with what they describe.

Adjectives ending in -**o** have four forms:		
m.	vino italian**o**	vini italian**i**
f.	birra italian**a**	birre italian**e**

Adjectives ending in -**e** have only two forms:		
m.	vino frances**e**	vini frances**i**
f.	birra frances**e**	birre frances**i**

3 **Articles** (the, a/an) have masculine and feminine forms.

	a/an	**the** singular	**the** plural	before . . .
m.	**un** giorno	**il** giorno	**i** giorni	consonant
	uno scontrino	**lo** scontrino	**gli** scontrini	**z**, **s**+consonant
	un anno	**l'**anno	**gli** anni	vowel
f.	**una** mela	**la** mela	**le** mele	consonant
	un'agenzia	**l'**agenzia	**le** agenzie	vowel

4 **The** combines with: **a** at/to; **da** from; **di** of; **in** in; **su** on.

	il	lo	l'	la	i	gli	le
a	al	allo	all'	alla	ai	agli	alle
da	dal	dallo	dall'	dalla	dai	dagli	dalle
di	del*	dello*	dell'*	della*	dei*	degli*	delle*
in	nel	nello	nell'	nella	nei	negli	nelle
su	sul	sullo	sull'	sulla	sui	sugli	sulle

*these words can mean 'some' as well as 'of the'

5 **Verbs** (words for doing or being) are easy to recognize in English because you can put 'to' in front of them: to live, to be, to speak, to pay, to have.

In Italian, the infinitive (the form you find in the dictionary) ends in: **-are**, **-ere** or **-ire**, each group following a pattern, with **-ire** verbs following one of two patterns.

		abit**are** to live	prend**ere** to take	part**ire** to leave	cap**ire** to understand
I	io	abit**o**	prend**o**	part**o**	cap**isco**
you	tu	abit**i**	prend**i**	part**i**	cap**isci**
you *s/he*	lei lei/lui	abit**a**	prend**e**	part**e**	cap**isce**
we	noi	abit**iamo**	prend**iamo**	part**iamo**	cap**iamo**
you	voi	abit**ate**	prend**ete**	part**ite**	cap**ite**
they	loro	abit**ano**	prend**ono**	part**ono**	cap**iscono**

6 Since the ending of the verb is enough to tell us who is doing something, the words for I, you, s/he, we, they are used in Italian only for emphasis, contrast or clarification of the you/he/she form.

7 There are three words for 'you' in Italian:

tu a friend, member of the family, young person
lei (often written **Lei**) someone you don't know well, someone older
voi more than one person

8 To say something **negative**, **non** goes in front of the verb:

Non parla inglese?   **Mario non è qui.**

9 The following are examples of some **irregular verbs** which do not follow the patterns and have to be learnt separately:

to		essere be	avere have	potere be able to	dovere to have to
I	io	sono	ho	posso	devo
you	tu	sei	hai	puoi	devi
you *s/he*	lei lei/lui }	è	ha	può	deve
we	noi	siamo	abbiamo	possiamo	dobbiamo
you	voi	siete	avete	potete	dovete
they	loro	sono	hanno	possono	devono

Verbs following **potere** and **dovere** are always in the infinitive.

Posso vedere?   **Deve cambiare.**

10 There are two written accents in Italian ´ and `. They are used to indicate a final stressed vowel, **città**, **caffè**, **ragù**, **perché**, or to distinguish between two words which otherwise look and sound the same, e.g. **da** from, **dà** give/s.

Italian–English glossary

This glossary contains all those words and phrases, and their meanings, as they occur in *Talk Italian*. Parts of verbs are given in the form in which they occur, usually followed by the infinitive in brackets.

A

a *to, at, in*
abbiamo (avere) *we have*
abitare *to live*
accordo: d'accordo *agreed, OK*
l' acqua *water*
l' acqua minerale *mineral water*
l' adulto *adult*
l' agenzia *agency*
l' aglio *garlic*
l' agnello *lamb*
agosto *August*
al, all', allo, ai, agli, alla, alle *at the, to the*
l' albergo *hotel*
l' alimentari (m.) *grocer's shop*
l' aliscafo *hydrofoil*
allora *then, well*
alto *high*
altro *other;*
Altro? *Anything else?*
l' amaro *bitter liqueur*
americano *American*
anche *also;* anch'io *me too*
andare *to go*
l' andata *single (ticket)*
l' andata e ritorno *return*
andiamo (andare) *we go, we're going, let's go*
l' anno *year*
l' antipasto *starter*
l' aperitivo *aperitif*
aperto *open*
l' appartamento *flat*
l' appetito *appetite;*
Buon appetito! *Enjoy your meal!*
aprile *April*
l' arancia *orange*

l' aranciata *orange drink*
archeologico *archeological*
l' architetto *architect*
arrivare *to arrive*
arrivederci *goodbye*
l' arrivo *arrival*
arrivo (arrivare) *I arrive*
arrosto *roast*
l' arte (f.) *art*
l' artista (m./f.) *artist*
l' ascensore (m.) *lift*
l' aspirina *aspirin*
assaggiare *to taste*
assortito *assorted*
l' attimo *moment*
l' Australia *Australia*
australiano *Australian*
l' autobus *bus*
avere *to have*
avete (avere) *you (pl.) have*
l' azienda di turismo *tourist office*

B

il bagno *bath, bathroom*
il bambino *child*
la banana *banana*
la banca *bank*
il bar *bar*
il barista *barman*
basso *low*
Basta *That's enough/all*
bene *well;*
Va bene *That's fine*
bere *to drink*
bianco *white*
la biblioteca *library*
il bicchiere *(drinking) glass*
il bigliettaio *ticket seller*
il biglietto *ticket*
il binario *platform*

la birra *beer*
la bistecca *steak*
bollito *boiled*
bolognese *from Bologna*
la bottiglia *bottle*
Bravo! *Well done!*
i broccoli *broccoli*
buona notte *good night*
buona sera *good evening*
buongiorno *hello*
buonissimo *very good indeed*
buono *good*

C

il caffè *coffee*
il caffelatte *milky coffee*
cambiare *to change*
il cambio *rate of exchange*
la camera *room*
la Camera di Commercio *Chamber of Commerce*
la campagna *country(side)*
il campeggio *campsite*
il campo da tennis *tennis court*
il Canadà *Canada*
canadese *Canadian*
capire *to understand*
capisco (capire) *I understand*
il cappuccino *frothy coffee*
il capretto *goat (kid)*
la caraffa *carafe*
caro *dear*
la carota *carrot*
la carta di credito *credit card*
la carta telefonica *phone card*
la cartolina *postcard*
la casa *house, home*
la casalinga *housewife*
casalinga *home-made*
casareccia *home-made*
la cassa *cash desk*

la cassiera (f.) *cashier*
il cassiere (m.) *cashier*
la categoria *category*
c'è *there is;*
    ce n'è uno/a *there is one
    (of them)*
la cena *dinner*
il centesimo *Italian currency*
il centro *centre*
il centro città *town centre*
il centro storico *old town*
la ceramica *ceramic*
il cerotto *sticking-plaster*
  certo *certainly*
  che *which, that, who*
  che *how;*
    che strano *How odd!*
  che? che cosa? *what?*
  chiamare *to call*
  chiamarsi *to be called*
la chiave *key*
il chilo *kilo*
  chiuso *closed*
  ci sono *there are*
  Ciao! *Hi; Bye*
  Cin cin! *Cheers!*
il cinema (m.) *cinema*
il cinghiale *wild boar*
il cioccolato *chocolate*
  cioè *that is*
la cipolla *onion*
la città *town, city*
la classe *class*
la coca *coke*
il cognome *surname*
la colazione, prima colazione
  breakfast
  come *how*
  completo *full*
  Complimenti *Congratulations*
  comprare *to buy*
la comunicazione
  communication
  con *with*
il coniglio *rabbit*
  consigliare *to recommend*
il contorno *side dish*
il controllo *control, check*
la conversazione *conversation*
il coperto *cover charge*

  corretto: caffè corretto
  coffee with alcohol
la cosa *thing;* che cosa? cosa?
  what? cos'è *what is it like?*
  così *so, like this/that*
  costa: quanto costa? *how
  much is (it)?* quanto costano?
  how much are (they)?
la cucina *cooking; kitchen*
la cugina (f.) *cousin*
il cugino (m.) *cousin*

D

dà; (dare) *give/s;* Mi dà
  Could you give me
  da *from*
  dal, dall', dallo, dai, dagli,
  dalla, dalle *from the*
la Danimarca *Denmark*
  del, dell', dello, dei, degli,
  della, delle *of the; some*
  delizioso *delicious*
il/la dentista *dentist*
  destra *right;*
    a/sulla destra *on the right*
  deve (dovere) *you must*
  devo (dovere) *I must*
  di *of; from*
  Dica/Mi dica (dire) *Can I
  help you?*
  dice (dire) *say/s;*
    Come si dice …? *How do
    you say …?*
  dicembre *December*
  dietro *behind*
  diretto *direct*
il direttore *manager*
  disoccupato *unemployed*
  dispiace: Mi dispiace *I'm sorry*
  divorziato *divorced*
la doccia *shower*
il dolce *dessert*
il dolcelatte *dolcelatte cheese*
la domenica *Sunday*
  doppio *double*
  dove *where;*
  dov'è? *where is?*
  dovere *to have to*
  dritto, sempre dritto
  straight on

il duomo *cathedral*

E

e *and*
  è (essere) *he/she/it is; you
  are*
  ecco *here is/are*
l' edicola *newspaper kiosk*
  Edimburgo *Edinburgh*
  esatto *exactly*
l' espresso *espresso coffee*
  essere *to be*
l' età *age*
l' etto *100 grams*
l' euro *euro*

F

  fa/fai (fare) *you do;*
    Che lavoro fa/fai? *What
    work do you do?*
  falso *false*
la famiglia *family*
la farmacia *chemist's shop*
  febbraio *February*
la fermata *(bus)stop*
  ferro: ai ferri *barbecued*
i figli *sons, children*
la figlia *daughter*
il figlio *son*
il filetto *fillet*
  finale *final*
  finalmente *finally, at last*
  fino a *as far as, until*
  fiorentino *from Florence,
  Florentine*
  Firenze *Florence*
il fondo *end, bottom;*
    in fondo *at the end of*
il formaggio *cheese*
  forno: al forno *baked*
  fra *between*
la fragola *strawberry*
  francese *French*
la Francia *France*
il francobollo *stamp*
il fratello *brother*
i fratelli *brothers (and sisters)*
  fritto *fried*
il frullato *milkshake*
la frutta *fruit*

fumatori *smoking*
il fungo *mushroom*
  ai funghi *with mushrooms*

G

la galleria *gallery*
il Galles *Wales*
  gallese *Welsh*
  gassata *sparkling;*
    non gassata *still*
il gelato *ice cream*
i gemelli *twins*
  gennaio *January*
la Germania *Germany*
il ghiaccio *ice*
il giardino *garden*
il giornale *newspaper*
il/la giornalista *journalist*
il giorno *day*
il giovedì *Thursday*
  girare *to turn*
  giugno *June*
  gli *the*
la Gran Bretagna *Britain*
la grappa *spirits*
  gratuito *free*
  grazie *thank you*
la Grecia *Greece*
  griglia: alla griglia *grilled*
la guida *guide, guidebook*

H

  ha (avere) *he/she has; you
  have*
  hai (avere) *you have*
  ho (avere) *I have*
l' hotel *hotel*

I

  i, il *the*
l' impiegato a (m./f.) *office
  worker*
  in *in, to*
  incluso *included*
l' indirizzo *address*
  industriale *industrial*
l' infermiera *nurse*
le informazioni *information,
  news*
l' ingegnere (m./f.) *engineer*

l' Inghilterra *England*
  inglese *English*
l' ingresso *entrance*
l' insalata *salad*
  integrale *whole;*
    pane integrale *wholemeal
    bread*
  io *I*
l' ipermercato *hypermarket*
l' Irlanda *Ireland*
  irlandese *Irish*
l' Israele *Israel*
l' Italia *Italy*
  italiano *Italian*

L

  la, l', le, lo *the*
  lasciare *to leave*
  lavorare *to work*
il lavoro *work, job*
  lei *you (formal), she*
  lentamente *slowly*
  lesso *boiled*
il letto *bed*
  lì *there, over there*
il litro *litre*
  lo *the, it;*
    non lo so *I don't know (it)*
  lontano *far*
  loro *they*
  luglio *July*
  lui *he*
il lunedì *Monday*
  lungo *long;*
    caffè lungo *coffee with
    added water*
il Lussemburgo *Luxembourg*
il lusso *luxury*

M

  ma *but*
  macchiato: caffè macchiato
    coffee with a dash of milk
la macedonia *fruit salad*
la madre *mother*
il magazzino *department store,
  warehouse*
  maggio *May*
il maiale *pig, pork*

il manzo *beef*
  marinara: alla marinara
  with seafood
il marito *husband*
il martedì *Tuesday*
  marzo *March*
  matrimoniale *double bedded
  (room)*
il medico *doctor*
la mela *apple*
il melone *melon*
il menù *menu*
il mercato *market*
il mercoledì *Wednesday*
il metro, metropolitana
  underground
  mezz'ora *half an hour*
  mezzo *half*
  mila *thousands*
  mille *one thousand*
la minestra *soup*
il minestrone *thick vegetable
  soup*
il minuto *minute*
  mio *my*
  misto *mixed*
  moderno *modern*
la moglie *wife*
  molti/e *many*
  molto *very; much;*
    molto/a *a lot of*
la mozzarella *mozzarella
  cheese*
il municipio *town hall*
il museo *museum*

N

la nazionalità *nationality*
  ne *of it, of them*
  necessario *necessary*
il negozio *shop*
  nel, nell', nello, nei, negli,
  nella, nelle *in the*
  niente *nothing, no*
  Nizza *Nice*
  No *No*
  noi *we*
il nome *name*
  non *not*

non-fumatori *non-smoking*
la nonna *grandmother*
i nonni *grandparents*
il nonno *grandfather*
la Norvegia *Norway*
la notte *night;*
   buona notte *good night*
novembre *November*
il numero *number*
il numero di telefono *phone number*

O

l' occupazione *occupation*
oggi *today*
ogni *every*
l' Olanda *Holland*
l' olio *oil;* olio di oliva *olive oil*
l' oliva *olive*
l' ora *hour, time*
ordinare *to order*
l' ospedale (m.) *hospital*
ottimo *excellent*
ottobre *October*

P

il padre *father*
il padrone *boss, proprietor*
il paese *country, village*
pagare *to pay*
il palazzo *palace, block of flats*
il pane *bread*
il panino *bread roll*
la panna *cream*
panoramica *panoramic*
parcheggiare *to park*
il parcheggio *car park*
parlare *to speak, to talk*
la partenza *departure*
partire *to leave*
il passaporto *passport*
il passo *step;*
   a due passi *very near*
la patata *potato*
   le patate fritte *chips*
la pensione *guesthouse;*
   pensione: in pensione *retired*
il pepe *pepper*
per *for*

per favore *please*
la pera *pear*
perché *because*
la periferia *outskirts, suburbs*
la pesca *peach*
il pesce *fish*
il petto *breast*
   piacciono: mi piacciono
   I like (them)
   piace: mi piace *I like (it)*
   Piacere *Pleased to meet you*
il piano *floor*
il pianterreno *ground floor*
la piantina *map*
il piatto *dish;*
   primo piatto *first course;*
   secondo piatto *main course*
la piazza *square*
la piazzola *place (in campsite)*
i piedi *feet;* a piedi *on foot*
la pineta *pine forest*
la piscina *swimming pool*
il pisello *pea*
   più *more, plus*
la pizza margherita *cheese and tomato pizza*
la pizzeria *pizza restaurant*
   poi *then*
il pollo *chicken*
il pomodoro *tomato*
il Portogallo *Portugal*
la posizione *position*
   possiamo (potere) *we can*
   posso (potere) *I can*
il posto *place, seat*
   potere *to be able to*
il pranzo *lunch*
   Prego *You're welcome; Can I help?*
   prendere *to take*
   prenotare *to book*
la prima colazione *breakfast*
la professione *profession*
il professore *teacher*
   pronto *ready*
   Pronto *Hello (on the phone)*
il prosciutto *ham*
   prossimo *next*
il pullman *coach*

il punto di controllo *checkpoint*
   può (potere) *he/she can; you can*

Q

quale? qual? *which?*
quando *when*
quanti? *how many?*
quanto? *how much?*
questo *this*
la questura *police headquarters*
qui *here*

R

il/la ragioniere *a accountant*
il ragù *bolognese sauce*
il rapido *fast train*
la regione *region*
il resto *change*
ripetere *to repeat*
il risotto *rice dish*
il ristorante *restaurant*
romano *Roman*
il rosmarino *rosemary*
rosso *red*

S

il sabato *Saturday*
il sale *salt*
Saluti *Regards, Greetings*
scendere *to get down, get off (bus/train)*
lo scontrino *receipt, ticket*
la Scozia *Scotland*
scozzese *Scottish*
scrive: Come si scrive? *How do you write it?*
scrivere *to write*
Scusi *Excuse me*
secondo *second*
la segretaria *secretary*
sei *six*
sei (essere) *you are*
il semaforo *traffic lights*
sempre *always*
senza *without*
la sera *evening;*
   buona sera *good evening*

settembre *September*
la settimana *week*
Sì *Yes*
siamo (essere) *we are*
la Sicilia *Sicily*
siciliano *Sicilian*
la signora *woman, Mrs, Madam*
il signore *man, Sir; signor Mr*
single *unmarried*
singola *single*
sinistra *left;*
  a/sulla sinistra *on the left*
so (sapere) *I know;*
  (io) non lo so *I don't know*
solo *only*
sono (essere) *I am; they are*
il sorbetto *sorbet*
la sorella *sister*
la Spagna *Spain*
spagnolo *Spanish*
la specialità *speciality*
lo spiedo *spit*
  allo spiedo *on a spit*
gli spinaci *spinach*
sposato *married*
la spremuta *freshly-squeezed orange juice*
squisito *excellent*
sta/i: Come sta/i? *How are you?*
la stagione *season*
stasera *this evening*
gli Stati Uniti *USA*
la stazione *station*
la sterlina *pound £*
strano *strange, odd*
lo studente *student*
lo studio *studio*
subito *immediately*

sul, sull', sullo, sui, sugli, sulla, sulle *on the*
suo *your; his, her*
il supermercato *supermarket*
il supplemento *supplement*
la Svizzera *Switzerland*
svizzero *Swiss*

T

la tabaccheria *tobacconist's shop*
la targa *car number plate*
il tavolo *table*
il tè *tea*
il teatro *theatre*
tedesco *German*
telefonare *to telephone*
il telefono *telephone*
terzo *third*
il tiramisù *Italian dessert*
la toilette *toilet*
la torta *cake, gateau*
tradizionale *traditional*
la tradizione *tradition*
il traghetto *ferry*
la trattoria *small family restaurant*
il treno *train*
tu *you (informal)*
il turismo *tourism*
tutti e due *both*
tutto *all*

U

l' ufficio *office*
l' ufficio postale *post office*
umido: in umido *stewed*
un, un', una, uno *one, a/an*
l' università *university*

le uova *eggs*
il' uovo *egg*

V

va bene *that's fine, OK*
la vacanza *holiday;*
  in vacanza *on holiday*
la valigia *suitcase*
vedere *to see*
vediamo (vedere) *let's see*
il venerdì *Friday*
veneziano *from Venice, Venetian*
verde *green*
la verdura *vegetables*
vergine *virgin*
vero *true*
la via *street*
viaggiare *to travel*
il viale *avenue*
vicino *near;* qui vicino *nearby*
il vigneto *vineyard*
la villetta *town house*
il vitello *veal*
voi *you (plural)*
volentieri *willingly, I'd love to/one*
volere *to wish, to want*
vorrei (volere) *I'd like*
vuole (volere) *you want*

Z

la zia *aunt*
lo zio *uncle*
la zona *area*
lo zucchero *sugar*
gli zucchini *courgettes*
la zuppa *soup*

Pathway to learning

BBC Worldwide publish a range of materials enabling you to continue to improve your Italian. For more information on our other titles visit our website: http://www.bbc.co.uk/learnlanguages or, to receive a catalogue, contact:

Bookpost
PO Box 29
Douglas
Isle of Man IM99 1BQ
Tel: 01624 675 137
Fax: 01624 670 923

BBC books are available at all good bookshops or direct from Bookpost as above.

For information on other language-learning support materials from the BBC, contact:

BBC Education Information
PO Box 1922
Glasgow G2 3WT
Tel: 08700 100 222
email: edinfo@bbc.co.uk

Other titles in the Talk . . . series include French, German, Greek, Japanese, Portuguese, Russian and Spanish.

Survival

Absolute Beginner

Beginner

Intermediate

Resources